JANE'S AIRCRAFT SPECTACULAR
HERCULES

Text by MIKE GAINES

Illustrations by JAMES GOULDING

JANE'S

First published in the United Kingdom in 1984 by
Jane's Publishing Company Limited,
238 City Road, London EC1V 2PU

ISBN 0 7106 0324 X

Distributed in the Philippines and the USA and its
dependencies by
Jane's Publishing Inc,
135 West 50th Street,
New York, NY 10020

Typeset by D. P. Media Ltd,
Hitchin, Hertfordshire

Printed by Toppan Printing Co Ltd,
Tokyo, Japan

James Goulding would like to thank J. S. Kellock (Marshall of Cambridge)
and Joe Dabney (Lockheed-Georgia) for their help with research material
for illustrations in this book.

Hercules on the battlefield: GIs double away from a C-130 during a combat assault exercise.

Hercules conception

Tanker, transport, bomber, reconnaissance, hospital, minelayer, maritime patrol, gunship, electronic surveillance, command post – these and other functions have all been performed by Lockheed's best-seller, the C-130 Hercules. The "Herc" has operated in the Himalayas, the Arctic, the Antarctic, and from a carrier. It has fought in the Congo, Vietnam, the Middle East and, most recently, in the South Atlantic. About the only thing it cannot do is talk but, with the current research into voice-operated cockpits, even that might come about one day, for the chances are that some variant of the C-130 will still be in production when the system is perfected.

In 1950, there were few aircraft designed specifically for handling cargo, a fact difficult to comprehend in the age of the dedicated cargo aircraft. The existing in-service types, the Douglas C-47 and C-54, were both designed as passenger aircraft, as were the Curtiss C-46 and the Douglas C-124 Globemaster. All were modified, to a greater or lesser extent, to accept bulky cargoes. Their structures were beefed up to take the loads, and the consequent increase in structural weight reduced their performance accordingly.

What the US Air Force and Army needed was a new start, with aircraft designed from the wheels up for the transport of bulky loads. Three categories were envisaged: a light, a medium, and a heavy or strategic transport. Each would overlap its partner to a certain extent, allowing greater operational flexibility.

In January 1951 the USAF's Tactical Air Command began conceptual studies for the medium-class transport, and on 2 February the Air Materiel Command issued requests for proposals to Boeing, Douglas, Fairchild and Lockheed.

At the time the Korean War was in full swing, with no end in sight. Fairchild's piston-engined C-119, although capable of rear loading, was slow and underpowered. There was a need for a fast, reliable, rugged aeroplane able to load quickly and unload even faster, either by air drop or on the ground, after landing on a rough strip. The requirements for fast loading and unloading were to dictate the fuselage shape, while speed and range requirements dictated the engine type and wing shape.

The shortcomings of types like Fairchild's C-119 Flying Boxcar prompted development of the Hercules.

The mission philosophy behind the design called for a classic all-out airborne assault operation. The first waves of aircraft would drop paratroopers who would take and hold a suitable stretch of ground. Howitzers, trucks, bulldozers and graders would then be dropped and a rough airstrip would be constructed. Successive waves would then fly in to the airstrip and land more supplies, equipment too heavy to drop, and troop reinforcements. Outgoing flights would evacuate battle casualties.

Lockheed was determined to beat rather than just meet the USAF's tough specifications. The project engineer for the Lockheed Temporary Design Designation L-206 was Art Flock, working under Willis Hawkins, head of the Advanced Design Department at Burbank, California. This department later produced the U-2, F-104 Starfighter and the SR-71, and is now working on a "Stealth"-technology fighter.

The USAF specified that the new transport should have a clear-cargo volume similar to a railway boxcar – 40 ft long, 10 ft wide and 9 ft high. The cargo floor had to be at the level of standard truck beds, allowing either roll-off/roll-on loading or the use of normal fork-lifts. An integral ramp and rear door, operable in flight, was also specified. The aircraft would be able to lift a 30,000 lb (13,608 kg) load over short intra-theatre distances or carry 90 troops or 64 paratroops for 2,000 nm (3,220 km). The large cargo compartment was to be pressurized to maintain a cabin altitude of 8,000 ft throughout the operating range.

The performance criteria represented a substantial jump from transports then in service. The one-engine-out performance over the drop zone was to be improved by a factor of 1.5 to 2. Design payload/range capabilities were multiplied by a factor of 8. The aircraft was to demonstrate "dependable" controllability and stability down to 125 kt for dropping, and at even lower speeds for rough/short strip landings on clay, sand or humus – what is now known as Stol (Short take-off or landing).

Starting with a blank sheet of paper and a headful of ideas, the Lockheed team went to work in a logical manner. So logical was the outcome that it is difficult to think of a better basic layout, as proved by the C.160 Transall, Antonov An-24, Shorts' Belfast and Skyvan, and the Aeritalia G.222.

Simplicity, reliability and ruggedness were the prime factors in the L-206 design. Secondary objectives were economy of manufacture, operation and maintenance. Simplicity and reliability could be enhanced by using the then-new turboprop engines instead of the relatively complicated and failure-prone piston engines. Another factor favouring turboprops was their good long-range, high-altitude performance. The one-engine-out requirement at high gross weight determined the need for four engines. The choice was the Allison T56-A-1, rated at 3,750 eshp and driving a Curtiss-Wright three-blade fully feathering and reversible-pitch propeller.

The call for long range at high altitude led to a high-aspect-ratio wing, while having the cargo floor at truck-bed level necessitated placing the wing high on the fuselage and keeping the carry-through box clear of the specified cargo volume. The wing span was 132 ft, with an aspect ratio of 10,

Hercules' cargo bay, looking aft and showing the black non-slip floor patches and rows of tie-down points.

giving a wing area of 1,745.5 ft² and a wing loading of 61.9 lb/ft² at the loaded weight of 108,000 lb.

After a few problems with flutter and undesirable vortices around the open ramp, windtunnel tests determined the correct shape and configuration for the cargo door. Hydraulically powered, the lower ramp was pushed down and the upper door folded inward for air dropping and ground access. The cone-section rear fuselage containing the ramp was transitioned to a flat elliptical section providing enough structural stiffness to carry the empennage.

The landing gear positioning posed a new set of problems. Conventional side-by-side two-wheel bogies on wing mounts were considered but discarded. On the high wing this arrangement would have been far too heavy. The obvious place to put the main gear was on the fuselage, but mounted in the now familiar blisters, thus keeping the all-important cargo volume free. Streamlining dictated the tandem arrangement of two large, low-pressure tyres to meet the soft-field landing requirements. The nose undercarriage, seemingly obvious in view of the rear-loading provision, was also of a high-flotation type. The Fairchild team arrived at a three-engined, tail-dragger configuration, similar in basic layout to the Junkers 52.

The cockpit was large and roomy, offering probably the best view of any aircraft other than helicopters. This was essential for accurate parachute dropping, formation flying, and more mundane things such as taxiing around bomb craters and other obstructions on front-line resupply missions. The crew was initially four: two pilots, a navigator and a flight engineer. This was later increased to five by the addition of an air loadmaster/dispatcher, leaving the flight engineer free to concentrate on the aircraft systems.

Systems-wise, the L-206 was not so much a step as a leap in the right direction as far as safety and ease of operation were concerned. In part the USAF requirement called for integral heating, cooling and ventilation, independent of the main engines. This need was fulfilled by an Auxiliary Gas Turbine mounted in front of the main trucks in the port wheel blister. The AGT also supplies high-pressure (HP) air to start the main engines and drive the Air Turbine Motor. Mounted above the AGT, the ATM drives a DC generator and an emergency hydraulic pump. The ATM and emergency hydraulic pump can also be driven by HP air bled from any of the main engines, either in the air or on the ground.

All flying controls were to be hydraulically boosted, with an unprecedented degree of system redundancy. Each control surface hydraulic booster was to have two separate and independent hydraulic systems. Each of the systems, known as the Boost System and the Utility System, was pressurized by two hydraulic pumps. The Boost System pumps are on engines 1 and 3 and the Utility System on engines 2 and 4. (Engines are numbered from port to starboard.) Any one engine pump can operate all three boosters (pitch, yaw and roll) under all normal flight conditions. As the name implies, the Utility System supplies pressure to operate the landing gear and flaps, the brakes and the nose gear steering.

Although the probability of complete Boost System failure was considered very low, Lockheed built in independent electrically operated trim tabs powered by the DC generator or the aircraft batteries. Should that fail, then the aircraft can be controlled at low speeds by the two pilots.

Lockheed even catered for this. As leg muscles are stronger than arm muscles, the bottom of the instrument panel is fitted with two foot bars against which the pilots can brace themselves to pull back the control columns. Emergencies apart, they make comfortable footrests for long transits on autopilot.

Although the cockpit layout looks conventional now, it was a masterpiece of applied ergonomics in 1951. The single power-control lever for each turboprop engine led to further simplification. Fuel and electrical control panels are designed to act as flow diagrams, making it easy to see at a glance which tank, for instance, is supplying which engines and by what route. The engine instruments are centrally mounted, giving both pilots and the engineer, who occupies a seat which slides on tracks behind them, a good view. Most engine and system controls are roof-mounted. The navigator sits on a swivel seat in the starboard side, and the port side contains a miniature galley. Fairly spartan toilet facilities are provided in the back of the cargo hold. On later-model aircraft one or two crew rest bunks are provided at the rear of the cockpit. With the hatch to the cargo door closed, the cockpit noise level is surprisingly low.

With autopilot engaged, this C-130 crew can relax a little and enjoy the superb view while sipping coffee and waiting for the next reporting point to appear under the nose.

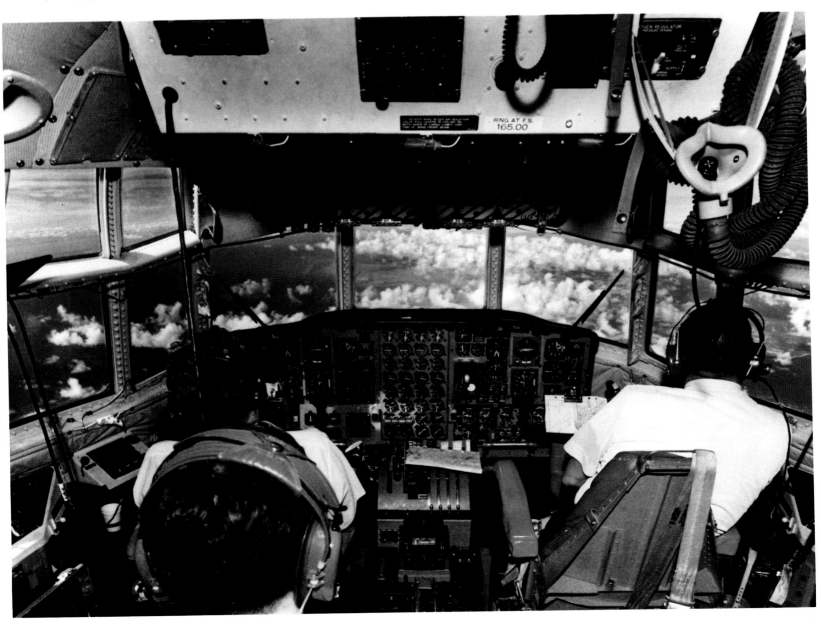

When published in February 1953 this first view of Lockheed's logical reshape of air transport caused a stir in aviation. The company's subsequent radical rethinks included the U-2, F-104 Starfighter and SR-71.

The second of the two YC-130A Hercules prototypes lifts off on its maiden flight from Burbank on 23 August, 1954. (Lockheed)

Weight saving

In April 1951, only two months after the RFP was issued, Lockheed submitted its L-206 design for USAF perusal. Extensive use of the new aluminium alloy A78S-T, able to absorb 7 per cent more allowable stress than the previously used A75S-T, kept the airframe weight down. Some 210 individual A78S-T parts would be used, a number of them weighing over 100 lb each. This new alloy allowed most weight savings, but metal bonding also helped, allowing thinner-gauge sheet to be used. Use of the then-new titanium for engine nacelles and flap skins saved 25 per cent in weight over their stainless steel equivalents.

The detail design and weight saving were worth the trouble. Lockheed exceeded the USAF requirements by a handsome margin. The predicted average cruising speed was 20 per cent better than required, ceiling and rate of climb at normal power were 35 per cent higher, one-engine-out ceiling and rate of climb were respectively 35 per cent higher and 55 per cent better than called for. Take-off distance at maximum power was 25 per cent better than needed, and landing distance, using brakes only – ie no reverse thrust – was 40 per cent shorter than the USAF had specified. All of this had been achieved while working around the key requirements of range and payload.

The USAF was understandably impressed and, on 2 July, 1951, Lockheed was named winner of the medium transport competition and awarded a contract for two YC-130 prototypes. Following its tradition of naming its types after stars and constellations, and reflecting on the strength of the Greek mythological hero, the company dubbed the type Hercules. The labours of Lockheed's Hercules were to make those of its Greek namesake seem small by comparison.

Flight trials – and tribulations

When it was rolled out at Burbank, California, in August 1954, the dumpy-looking YC-130A created something of a sensation in the aeronautical Press. Lockheed had a name (and still does) for producing sleek, elegant designs such as the P-38 Lightning and the Constellation airliner. But, to be polite, the YC-130 could not be called anything but workmanlike. Indeed, it is said that Kelly Johnson, who later headed the design of the F-104 Starfighter, the U-2 and the SR-71, refused to append his name to Lockheed's original proposal to the US Air Force.

Work on two YC-130A prototypes was started in August 1951 at Lockheed's Burbank plant. While construction of the prototypes continued, Lockheed executives decided that, should all go well and a C-130 production contract be awarded, the aircraft would be built by the Lockheed-Georgia subsidiary company at Marietta, Georgia. Accordingly, engineers from Marietta were transferred to Burbank to work on the prototypes some three days after Lockheed received a letter of intent from the US Air Force for seven C-130As.

Work progressed smoothly on the prototypes and on a wooden full-scale engineering mockup. The mockup was transferred by ship, via the Panama Canal, to Savannah, Georgia, in September 1953, completing its journey to Marietta by road.

The Marietta factory was originally built to churn out Boeing B-29s in World War Two. Closed on VJ Day, it was used as a warehouse until 1951, when it re-opened to refurbish mothballed B-29s for the Korean War. Later Boeing awarded Lockheed-Georgia a contract to licence-build B-47 Stratojets. The company eventually rolled out 394 B-47s and then gave money *back* to the Government. So efficient was the Marietta operation that some of the money allocated to build B-47s "was not needed".

Marietta's B-47 production engineer, Al Brown, was named Project Engineer for the C-130. He and 40 production specialists moved to Burbank to work on the prototypes. Later, several Lockheed-California employees were to move to Georgia with the C-130 programme. Some moves were temporary, other employees still live there.

Back at Burbank the second prototype, 33397, was ready for its first flight on 23 August, 1954. The pilot was Stan Beltz, his copilot was Roy Wimmer, and flight-test engineers Dick Stanton and Jack Real completed the crew. The take-off

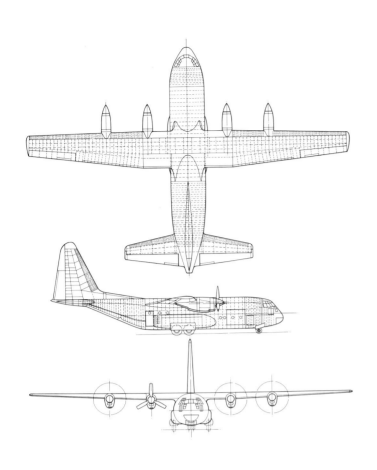

First of the many. The configuration set by the YC-130A has changed little over the subsequent years of development apart from the addition of the characteristic radome "pimple" to the snub profile shown here.

The first inkling of the Herc's sparkling performance came when the photo-chase P-2 Neptune had trouble in keeping up, especially in the climb. (Lockheed)

was scheduled for 0900, but the Los Angeles area was shrouded in a thick layer of smog and the maiden flight was postponed. Slightly disappointed, the test crew retired to the factory for coffee and to sit out the smog.

Five hours later the smog lifted and the flight was on. The crew taxied out to the runway, getting used to the aircraft's bounding gait, which gave them the impression of being in a small boat on a large swell. Beltz pushed the power levers forward and accelerated down the runway. After allowing the nose gear to unstick he reversed the propellers' pitch and brought the Hercules to a stop. Turning around, he performed the same manoeuvre in the opposite direction, getting the feel of the aircraft.

After a pause to allow the chase aircraft to take off the YC-130 again lined up. Beltz stood on the brakes and put the Hercules at full power. The prototype bounced around on its gear, eager to be away. At 2.45 pm Beltz let the brakes off. The crowd of watching Lockheed workers and VIPs were astonished. Eight seconds and 855 ft from brakes-off the YC-130A was airborne and climbing fast at a 30° angle.

Beltz and his crew arrived at 10,000 ft somewhat faster than they were used to with four-engine transports. The landing gear and flaps were cycled, the aircraft's general handling was explored, and a series of stalls was made, noting the airspeed with different configurations, both the "clean" aircraft and with gear and flaps down.

No major problems came to light, and Beltz headed out over the Sierra Nevada mountains to Edwards AFB,

home of the Air Force Flight Test Center, where the YC-130 would be based for test flying. On landing, Beltz and his crew were little short of ecstatic. "When we took off it wanted to climb so bad I had trouble keeping the airspeed down. She's a real flying machine," he said. After the fairly short landing Beltz confided to the AFFTC's commander that "I could land her crossways of the runway if I had to."

However, the C-130 test programme was not without its problems. The biggest snag to be overcome was with the engine-propeller interface. The Allison T56 turbine was not a problem. All it had to do was keep turning at a constant speed. Linked through reduction gearboxes, the Curtiss-Wright propellers also turned at a constant 1,108 rpm. To alter the available power, the pitch of the propeller blades was changed. To produce more thrust the blades were twisted about their axes to take a larger "bite" of air. This simplified life in the cockpit, combining the instantly available changes in thrust usually associated with piston engines with the benefits of a jet engine's reliability, smoothness, and fuel economy in high-level cruise.

The problem was with the automatic pitch governor. To keep engine speed constant, the governor, which was triggered by electrical signals, should have increased pitch as fuel flow increased. In some cases, however, the governor would over-compensate, then over-compensate the other way. This "hunting" was transmitted to the propeller, which would increase and decrease pitch accordingly. The effect was to overheat, and in some cases wreck, the reduction gearboxes and rapidly increase and decrease thrust on the affected propeller.

In flight this meant a jerky progression, with the aircraft's nose jerking around as the thrust on one side increased and decreased. It all happened so fast that the pilot was unable to compensate. On several occasions the oscillations grew so violent that the offending propeller had to be feathered and the engine closed down.

By this time the tenth production C-130A was coming off the line at Marietta. Both the US Air Force and Lockheed were wary of going any further with the "electric" propellers. The aircraft could not go into service with such a fault, and there was not enough time to fix the snag before production got into full swing. The service and the company decided to change to hydraulically driven propellers and selected a new design by Aero Products, a division of the engine makers, Allison.

Later, with the C-130B, the propeller was again changed. A competition for the new propeller was then won by a new Hamilton four-blader. The Curtiss-Wright propeller governor was later sorted out, but by then the C-130As had all been retrofitted with the three-blade Aero Products variety.

The propeller had nothing to do with the infamous engine fire of the third Hercules. Given construction number 3001, the first production-standard C-130A was rolled out from the Marietta factory on 10 March, 1955. A month later, on 7 April, the production C-130A was flown from Lockheed's Marietta airfield, a joint facility with Dobbins Air Force Base (AFB). Again the acceleration and rate of climb astounded the onlookers, mainly company employees. After an 800 ft groundroll test pilot Leo Sullivan rotated the nose and gave the Hercules its head, passing over the end of the 10,000 ft-long runway at 2,500 ft. A week later Sullivan and his crew were to run from the aircraft as it burned on the same runway.

On 14 April Sullivan and his crew had been airborne on the aircraft's third flight, an air-to-air photographic session over nearby Stone Mountain followed by calibrated speed runs. During the return to base the flight engineer, Ed Shockley, noticed a slight fluctuation in the fuel flow to the port inner (Number Two) engine. Simultaneously, witnesses on the Cobb Parkway just outside the airfield saw greyish smoke or vapour coming from the engine. As the propellers were brought back into reverse pitch on touchdown the fuel vapour was drawn forward to envelop the hot exhaust of the engine, which burst into flames.

Sullivan closed down both starboard engines and turned off the runway on to the grass. The engine fire extinguishers failed to douse the flames, however, and the test crew made a rapid exit. Despite the fast reaction of both Lockheed and Dobbins AFB fire crews the raging fire burnt through the mainspar and the port wing snapped between the seat of the fire in Number Two and the wing root. The first production C-130 was a sorry sight, covered with foam and dragging its broken wing in the grass.

An investigation later showed that a connector on the engine fuel line had vibrated loose after incorrect assembly. A modification was devised to make the connector "Murphy-proof" so that it would no longer be possible to assemble it wrongly. The aircraft was re-winged and flying again within a few months.

Aerodynamically, there was little wrong with the Hercules. It was found to be remarkably light and responsive for its size, yet it could be placed in a turn and would stay there. This controllability, coupled with the power of the four Allison T56s, certainly made the Hercules a pilot's aeroplane. Everyone who has flown the Hercules has commented favourably on its handling qualities.

One potentially serious fault that showed up was a structurally weak tailplane. The load distribution across the span of the tailplane was found to be greater outboard than planned for, buckling the tailplane and causing the elevators

The first production "Charlie One-Thirty" takes shape at Lockheed's Marietta plant, with the Boeing B-47 Stratojet line still going strong in the background.　　(Lockheed)

The second production C-130A never flew, being used instead as the structural testbed. Here it undergoes cabin/hold pressure integrity tests in a water tank.　　(Lockheed)

to flutter asymmetrically. Lockheed beefed up the internal structure starting with the C-130B, and A models were limited to 287 kt. To be fair to both Lockheed and its Hercules, the problem was first noted when test pilot Leo Sullivan pushed the nose down into a −0.5 g bunt at 340 kt. This corner of the flight envelope would not normally be explored by the average squadron pilot.

The second production C-130A was selected as the static test airframe. Doomed never to fly, it was covered in strain gauges and pummelled by hydraulic rigs to simulate thousands of hours' flying and dozens of take-offs and landings. The aircraft, in sections, was later immersed in a water tank, where the fuselage pressurization was tested for weak points.

Flight and ground testing proved to the Air Force what they already knew: Lockheed build good, reliable and rugged aeroplanes. With the possible exception of the C-130 the company also builds good-looking aircraft, but in operational service the Hercules was to prove that looks aren't everything.

This Indonesian Air Force C-130-MP is seen dropping rescue kit from the ramp. Note the observation door.

(Lockheed)

Above Middle Eastern Herc club members include Abu Dhabi, which operates four C-130Hs as part of the multi-national United Arab Emirates Air Force. Dubai contributes to the UAEAF with an L-100-30. (Lockheed)

Below After Israel and Iran, Egypt has the largest Hercules fleet in the Middle East. (Lockheed)

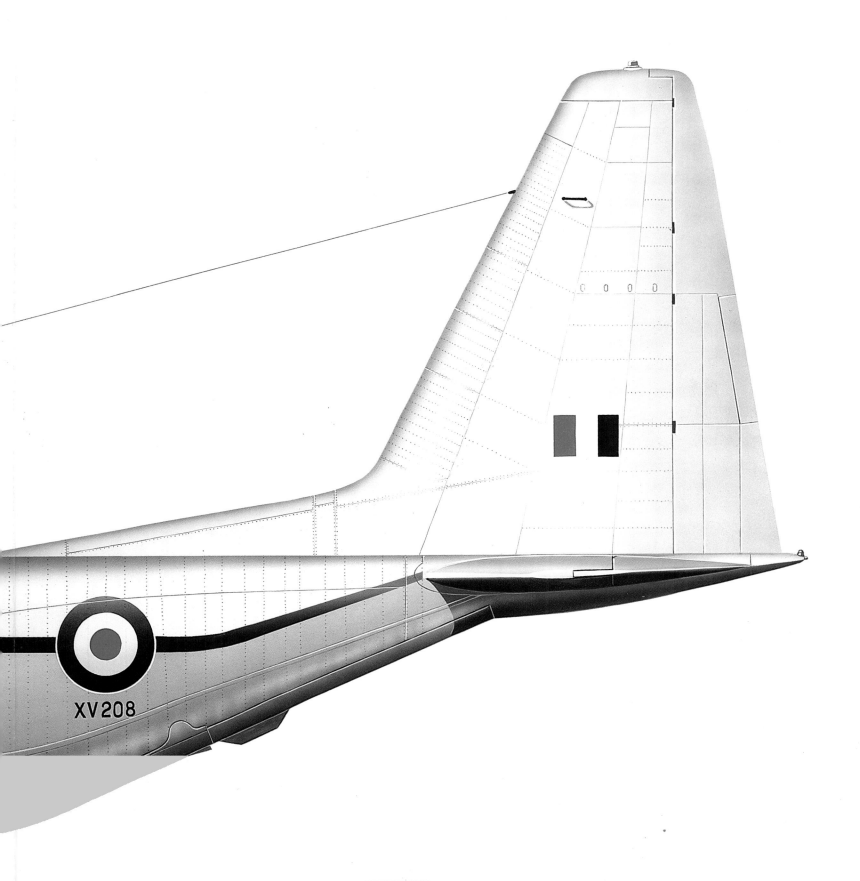

XV208

James Goulding.

After Vietnam most of the gunship Hercules were transferred to various Air Force Reserve (AFRes) or Air National Guard (ANG) units, since the likelihood of their being needed in anger again seemed remote. But Spooky is now enjoying a revival and seems set to continue. Indeed, more Hercules might yet be converted to gunship configuration. Besides being held in readiness to cover the withdrawal of the ill-fated Delta Force in the Iran rescue mission, the gunships again proved their worth in Operation Urgent Fury, the invasion of Grenada. Hercules gunships flew defence-suppression missions, while standard C-130Hs dropped paratroops of the 82nd and 101st Airborne divisions. One interesting infantry fire-support call came when a platoon was pinned down by heavy-calibre machine-gun fire from the Cubans. The platoon's radio was smashed, so a quick-thinking GI used his American Express card to telephone the headquarters for the operation, at Fort Bragg, North Carolina. The gunship was alerted and the target co-ordinates successfully passed by satellite, and the machine-gun nest was wiped out in one firing pass.

AC-130H Pave Spectre II leading data

Mission Close air support

Powerplant Four Allison T56-A-15 turboprops, flat-rated to 4,508 ehp

Armament Two M61 20 mm cannon mounted forward, two MXU-470 7.62 mm minigun modules mounted midships, M2A1 40mm cannon at aft end of landing gear sponson, and 105 mm gun mounted in place of rear paratroop exit. All guns face port

Avionics AN/APN-59B search radar in nose, AN/AVQ-21 port-mounted pilot's gunsight system, AN/ASD-5 direction-finder set (Black Crow, detects vehicle ignition systems), AN/ASQ-15 low-light-level TV, AN/AAD-7 infra-red detector set, AN/APQ-150 beacon tracking radar, AN/AVQ-17 2 kW searchlight, AN/AVQ-19 laser target designator/ranger, AN/AJQ-24 stabilized tracking set, AN/ALR-46 radar warning receivers, AN/ALQ-87 electronic countermeasures (ECM) pods carried on inboard wing stations (other ECM pods also available according to mission requirements), and SUU-42 infra-red countermeasures (IRCM) pods on outboard pylons (other IRCM pods available)

Dimensions
Wing span 132 ft 7 in (40.41 m)
Length overall 97 ft 9 in (34.37 m)
Height overall 38 ft 3 in (11.66 m)
Wing area 1,745 ft² (162.12 m²)

Weights
Empty 76,469 lb (34,686 kg)
Max take-off (overload) 175,000 lb (79,380 kg)

Performance
Maximum speed 325 kt
Service ceiling 33,000 ft

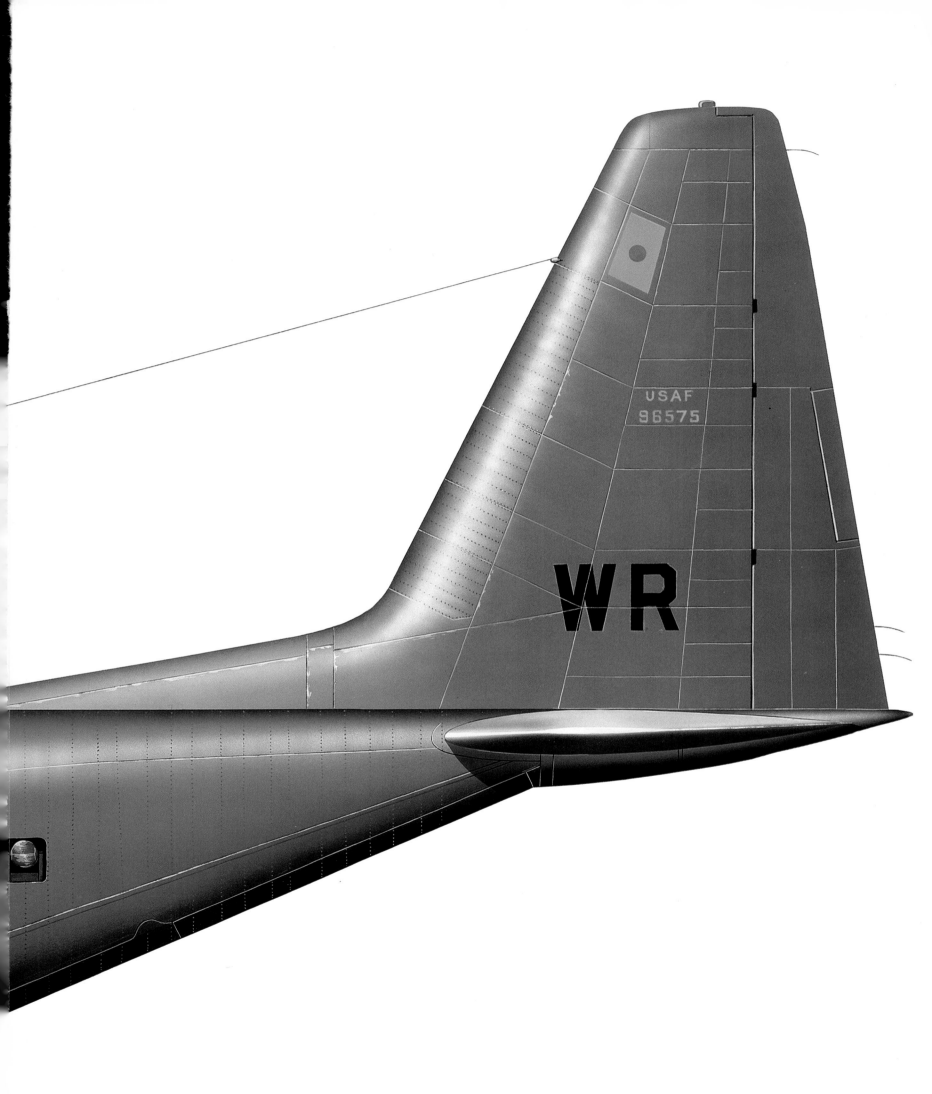

USAF
96575

WR

James Goulding

Operated by the Royal Aircraft Establishment's Meteorological Research Flight based at Farnborough, Hercules W.2 XV208 is a unique aircraft and probably the best-equipped weather research vehicle in the world. Converted from an RAF Hercules C.1 by Marshall of Cambridge, XV208 first flew in W.2 form on 21 March, 1973. The 18ft nose boom carries highly sensitive yaw/pitch vanes, a pitot-static head, and two air-temperature sensors. The long boom necessitated mounting the Ekco 280 weather radar in a pod offset slightly to starboard above the flightdeck. Two forward-facing TV cameras are mounted just below the pilot's windshield, and a third camera is fitted internally to look through the windshield. The monitoring crew are accommodated in a "scientific pod" in the cargo hold. Other modifications include an electronically controlled, hydraulically powered ejection rack on the rear ramp for up to 60 radio drop-sondes. The two outboard wing pods can carry a variety of sensor and telemetry equipment. The aircraft is used to monitor and research atmospheric phenomena throughout the world, and regularly penetrates tropical storms such as hurricanes.

Lockheed Hercules W.2 leading data

Mission Meteorological research

Powerplant Four Allison T56-A-15 turboprops, flat-rated to 4,508 ehp

Armament None

Avionics Ekco 280 weather radar, Omega INS, 60 radio drop-sondes and associated telemetry, Barnes radiation thermometer, three forward-facing TV cameras

Dimensions
Wing span 132 ft 7 in (40.41 m)
Length overall 120 ft (36.58 m)
Height overall 38 ft 5 in (11.71 m)
Wing area 1,745 ft² (162.12 m²)

Weights
Empty 70,678 lb (32,059 kg)
Max take-off 155,000 lb (70,310 kg)

Performance
Maximum speed 325 kt
Service ceiling 33,000 ft
Range 4,500 nm

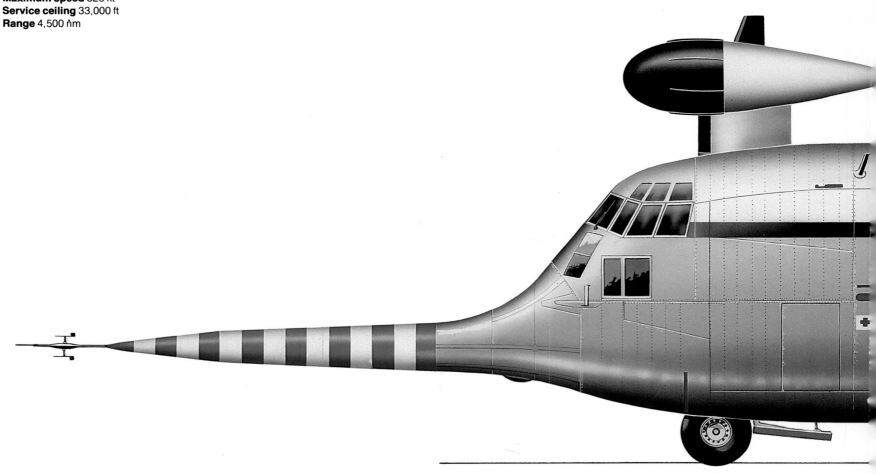

Into service

The first delivery of the Hercules to a US Air Force operational squadron was made on 9 December, 1956, when five C-130As were flown in to Ardmore, Oklahoma, and handed over to Tactical Air Command's 463rd Troop Carrier Wing. The first aircraft to land was 55023, named *City of Ardmore* after the base's local town. This aircraft is still in service, flying with the Illinois Air National Guard from O'Hare Airport, Chicago. It therefore follows that some of the C-130s coming off the line today could be in service until the year 2008, or probably longer, as the later models are built of tougher alloys.

The Herc's first missions were mainly concerned with shuttling troops and National Guardsmen around the southern states from one trouble spot to another, owing to civil unrest resulting from the desegregation of black and white universities and schools. But this inauspicious start allowed the 463rd's crews to fly the aircraft on real operations instead of training exercises, and many useful lessons were learnt.

The Hercules was popular with its crews from the start, proving easy and comfortable to fly, with lots of performance in hand. Its crews delighted in the querulous radio calls from fighter jocks who wanted to know what a dumpy-looking propeller-driven aircraft was doing at 35,000 ft. Although it was considered noisy by later generations of aircrew, the C-130's flightdeck was a lot quieter than those of its predecessors. Ask anyone who flew either the Douglas C-124 Globemaster or the Handley Page Hastings – he probably still won't be able to hear the question.

The C-130A's excess of power and excellent handling qualities were demonstrated by four 463rd TCW crews at Ardmore when they formed the first C-130 "aerobatic" team. Known as the "The Four Horsemen", the team started its display with a high-speed flypast in diamond-four formation after a two-second stream take-off. From the fly-by the team pulled up into a diamond-four wingover, changing to a close-formation tail chase. After performing high- and low-speed passes and wingovers in trail and echelon formations, the Horsemen reformed in diamond for a high-speed run and break. On the break the leader and box man pulled up and turned 45° right and left respectively while the two wingmen pulled into 90° outward turns. The aircraft then spaced on the downwind legs for alternate left and right final turns into short landings.

A similar but less extensive display was put on by three Hercules of the 317th Tactical Airlift Wing at RAF Mildenhall's 1981 air show in England.

In US Air Force service the Hercules soon gained a reputation that was the envy of the rest of the world, and the slow but steady overseas sales started in 1957 with an order from the Royal Australian Air Force for 12 C-130As. Indonesia and Canada soon followed with orders for ten and four aircraft respectively. Other countries followed suit. Canada, impressed with its first four C-130Bs, placed two repeat orders for 20 and four aircraft respectively, choosing the more powerful C-130E. But the United Kingdom placed

First production C-130A to be delivered (**top**) to an operational unit was *City of Ardmore*, one of five aircraft assigned to the 463rd Troop Carrier Wing at Ardmore AFB, Oklahoma, on 9 December, 1956. The 3050 on the nose is Lockheed's construction number. Tail-numbered 50023, *City of Ardmore* is still in service with the Air Force Reserve's 928th Tactical Airlift Group, based at Chicago O'Hare International Airport. The old stager poses (**above**) over Chicago's Grant Park.

the largest overseas order to date. In 1965 the Royal Air Force selected the Hercules as its Beverley/Hastings replacement, ordering 66 aircraft.

The RAF version was the C-130K. Almost identical to the C-130H, the C-130K entered service in 1967 as the Hercules C.1. As part of the industrial offset for such a large order some airframe components were made by Scottish Aviation (now British Aerospace, Scottish Division) at Prestwick. The UK-manufactured components were then flown to Georgia for incorporation into the RAF's aircraft on the production line. At one point thought was given to building RAF Hercules with Rolls-Royce Tyne engines as an additional offset, but this idea was dropped and the usual Allison T56-A-15s were used.

However, the RAF's C-130s were fitted with British avionics and flightdeck instrumentation. This was done as much in the interest of commonality as for offset. The C-130s were delivered to Marshall of Cambridge unpainted. At Cambridge Airport they were sprayed in the RAF's chocolate and sand "mid-east" camouflage scheme with gloss black undersides and a heat-reflecting white roof to the cockpit. Marshalls also fitted the British systems. The company is still involved with RAF Hercules, carrying out all major servicing and modifications.

The first modification was to remove the astrodome fitted on RAF Hercs. The decision to revert to the standard periscope sextant was taken after two of the domes failed under pressure. This was potentially very dangerous. Had a navigator been taking an astro shot at the time, he could have been sucked out by the rapid decompression.

Marshalls were also responsible for the major rebuild of one Royal Air Force aircraft into the Royal Aircraft Establishment's Hercules W.2. This turned the standard transport variant into an extremely valuable scientific tool. The sole Hercules W.2 is operated by the RAE's Meteorological Research Flight.

To obtain accurate data on air pressure and temperature the aircraft needed a long boom to keep the sensor heads clear of interference caused by the aircraft itself. The 22 ft boom was mounted on the nose, this being the only place where it would be comparatively vibration-free. The radar aerial was moved to a pod mounted above the cockpit, and two telemetry and air-sampling pods were mounted under the outer wing panels. The cargo hold was modified to take banks of sensitive scientific and recording equipment in a special pod designed to minimize vibration. The cargo ramp was fitted with launch tubes for radio sondes. Acting like aerial sonobuoys, these transmit data on the surrounding atmosphere as they fall by parachute. Other buoys are dropped into the sea to obtain data on water temperature, which affects the weather.

The Hercules W.2 spends much of its time abroad, making long flights through what the crews describe as "interesting" weather systems. This can mean anything from penetrating a cumulo-nimbus to flying through the eye of tropical storms, all the while sensing and recording the environment outside.

Another 30 of the Royal Air Force's C-130Ks are being stretched by Marshalls to C-130H-30 standard, whereupon they are re-designated Hercules C.3. More importantly, in terms of airlift power this gives the RAF the equivalent of ten more Hercules C.1s. The 15 ft stretch enables seven standard pallets to be carried instead of the Hercules C.1's five. Alternatively it provides room for 128 troops instead of 92, or for 92 paratroops instead of 64. For casualty evacuation the C-130H-30/Hercules C.3 can uplift 93 stretcher cases and six medical attendants – 23 more patients than can be evacuated by a standard C-130.

Hercules development

Although external changes to the basic transport variant are minimal, the Hercules has benefited from many invisible improvements. It is this constant rejuvenation that makes the Hercules a best-seller both now and in the foreseeable future.

Lockheed and the US Air Force were understandably pleased with the C-130A, of which 204 were built: 192 for the USAF and 12, with T56-A-12 engines, for the Royal Australian Air Force. But the manufacturer was not content to rest on its laurels, and design work on the more powerful B model was already in hand.

The C-130B was first flown on 20 November, 1958. The B was re-engined with Allison T-56-A-7s rated at 4,050 shp and driving the standardized four-blade, 13.5 ft-diameter propellers. The new powerplants enabled the B's weight to grow to 135,000 lb from the 124,200 lb of the A. Although the B's maximum payload was only 34,840 lb, compared with the A's 35,000 lb, the later model carried more fuel. The A's external 900 gal tanks were deleted and extra internal tanks were added inboard of the engines. The B's total fuel capacity was 6,960 gal, compared with the A's 6,150 gal, giving greater payload range. But the heavier B was less nimble than its earlier counterpart, the wing loading having crept up from 71.2 lb/ft² to 77.4 lb/ft². All B models had the "droop snoot" radome, which was fitted as standard from the 28th C-130A onwards.

The C-130B's longer range dictated the provision of crew rest facilities. Accordingly, a double bunk was fitted at the rear of the cockpit, enabling two men to sleep on a long flight. The galley was also improved and expanded slightly. In anticipation of the greater loads to come, the B model's undercarriage was strengthened, enabling the aircraft to withstand a 9 ft/sec sink rate at 118,000 lb on landing. The C-130A's maximum landing weight at a similar velocity was only 96,000 lb.

Take-off at 100,000 lb was achieved from 2,000 ft of runway, but even this could be reduced by the addition of eight 1,000 lb-thrust rocket-assisted take-off (Rato) bottles affixed to the rear of the main gear sponsons. The first C-130B was delivered in December 1958. Lockheed were to build 123 B models for the US Air Force and 33 for overseas sales.

The C-130E, first flown on 15 August, 1961, represented a massive jump in payload/range capability for the Hercules. The A and B models were optimized for tactical transport. With the E Lockheed shifted the design-point philosophy more towards long-range supply to ordinary airfields, but retained the rough-field capability of the earlier Hercules models. The basic weight was increased to 155,000 lb, 2,000 lb more than the B model and 30,800 lb more than the A model.

The payload was increased to 45,579 lb, while the total fuel jumped at 9,680 gal, compared with 6,960 gal on the B and 6,150 gal on the A model. Of the increased fuel volume, 6,960 gal was carried internally as on the B. The extra 2,720 gal was accommodated in two massive underwing external tanks, pylon-mounted between the engines. The weight of the external fuel also helped relieve the bending moment put on the wings by the increased payload. The forward cargo door was deleted from all C-130s after the first eight C-130Es.

The engines remained the same as the C-130B's, however, and combined with another increase in wing

Above Blunt-nosed C-130As with small tanks outboard of the engines are rare these days. This example is named for Nashville and serves with the Tennessee Air National Guard.

Right Even more rare are C-130As with three-blade propellers. This much modified example is a JC-130A which has also seen life as an AC-130A. (USAF)

Below right This immaculate C-130B is seen here in the markings of the 6593rd Test Squadron of Air Force Systems Command.

Bottom right The Royal Air Force originally specified a transparent astrodome for its C-130Ks. This idea was later dropped after a couple of the domes cracked at high altitude: luckily, no navigators were ejected. This Lyneham-based Herc shows the current standard. (MoD)

Below The L-100-30 and its Royal Air Force equivalent, the C.3, represent the longest stretch yet of the basic Hercules airframe. The RAF version is also equipped for air-to-air refuelling.

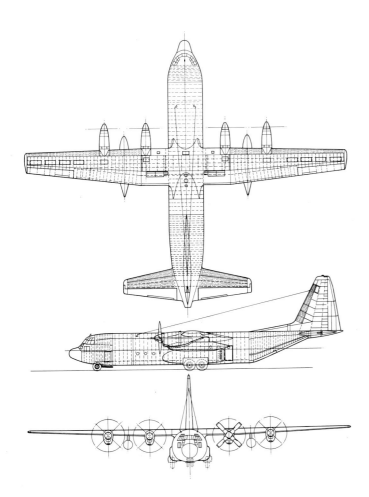

loading, this time to 88.8 lb/ft², made the C-130E more sluggish than the C-130B, although there was still power to spare.

Able to carry 35,000 lb of cargo non-stop to Europe or cross the Pacific with only one refuelling stop, the C-130E relieved the US Air Force of many worries over landing rights when performing its increasingly global role. A few years after its entry into US Air Force service in April 1962, the C-130E was to prove invaluable in south-east Asia. Lockheed produced 377 C-130E variants for the USAF, one EC-130E for the US Navy, and four basically similar C-130Gs for the US Coast Guard. The Marietta factory was also to produce 111 C-130Es for nine other countries.

The C-130H is basically the same as the C-130E, but has more powerful T56-A-15 engines derated from 4,910 shp to 4,508 shp and improved braking, hydraulics, avionics and air-conditioning systems. All C-130Hs produced since 1969 have a redesigned wing centre box assembly, and this has been retrofitted to earlier Hercules. The new wing section has been rig-tested to 40,000 hr. As the average C-130 utilization rate is 700 hr a year, the aircraft will be flying for a long time yet.

The H model was also given a more modern auxiliary power unit. The APU, which needed a 20 in extension to the main gear sponson to accommodate it, doubles the electrical output to 40 kVA. Other benefits of the new APU are a 34 per cent increase in air supply with a seven per cent pressure increase, and a shortening of engine start time. The APU eliminates the air turbine motor previously needed, and has a mean time between failures (MTBF) of 1,500 hr, compared with 200 hr of the earlier-type APU.

The higher-capacity APU enabled Lockheed to fit an improved and more reliable air-conditioning system in the H model. Earlier C-130s had one 70 lb/min-flow unit and a 30 lb/min unit. On the C-130H there are two 70 lb/min units made of longer-lifed materials and with slower-running turbines. The benefits are better cooling on the ground and at low level, with better ventilation. If one unit should become unserviceable, then the other can maintain the temperature at

a comfortable level. The units can also transfer conditioned air from the flightdeck to the cargo hold and vice versa. This is a valuable flight safety feature. Should toxic fumes emanate from badly packed cargo, then the cargo-hold air can be "dumped overboard" while a separate system handles the cockpit environment. Both of the air-conditioning units are much more reliable than the old type, with MTBFs of 20,000 hr, compared with 300 hr on their predecessors.

On the flightdeck the C-130H was given a new Automatic Flight Control System (AFCS). Smaller and 111 lb lighter than previous models, the solid-state Collins AP-105 was also found to be four times more reliable, besides being cheaper and more versatile.

The AN/APN-59 weather and search radar was

Right The HC-130H was originally equipped to snatch downed aircrew by picking up a balloon-borne line in the nose yoke, shown here folded back.

Below Hercules doing what it was actually designed for, supplying the army in the field. In this case a C-130E demonstrates the spectacular but efficient Low Altitude Parachute Extraction System.

replaced by the more modern AN/APQ-122 with twice the range and higher sensitivity. The MTBF of the new solid-state radar is 260 hr, compared with the 50 hr of the old type.

Handling is improved on the H, with a dual hydraulic system powering twin rudder actuators arranged in series. The three original hydraulic systems – utility, boost and emergency – were all simplified for improved reliability.

The brakes were replaced by high-energy, tri-metallic, multi-disc Goodyear units with 60 per cent more stopping power than the old type. Weighing only 30 per cent more, the new disc brakes are able to absorb 60 per cent more heat than the old units, allowing ten times more landings before replacement is necessary. A new Hytrol II anti-skid system was fitted to the brakes, enabling C-130Hs to land safer and shorter than earlier Hercules. The C-130H has demonstrated a 1,200 ft ground roll at 100,000 lb landing weight.

To sum up the differences in performance between the C-130A and the C-130H, the H has 20 per cent more power, lifts 26 per cent more payload over 52 per cent more range 11 per cent faster than the A models. The fuel capacity has gone up by 57 per cent, and the airframe life is twice that of the earlier aircraft.

Assault Hercules: the C-130J

With the exception of later stretched variants the C-130H was the last basic model change to the Hercules. However, Lock-

heed did propose another basic model – the C-130J Assault Hercules. Based on early experience with the C-130s in Vietnam, the C-130J was optimized for assault landings on an unprepared strip under small-arms fire.

Lockheed design staff studied operations in Vietnam and decided to design the C-130J around a 25,000 lb payload mission over a radius of 500 nm. The first 400 nm would be flown at cruise altitude and speed, while the last 100 nm was to be flown at 100 ft and 270 kt. It was supposed that ground fire could be expected within a 50 nm radius of the destination. The strip was assumed to be rough and with a load-bearing quality and friction similar to that of a wet lawn.

The soft and rough airfield imposed requirements that could not be met with the existing C-130 undercarriage, so a new undercarriage was designed. Each wheel of the main gear would have 25 in double-stroke articulated oleos with fatter tyres. At 130,000 lb landing weight the C-130J would be able to absorb a sink rate of 17 ft/sec, compared with the 9 ft/sec tactical landing of normal C-130s. The nose undercarriage leg would also be of double-stroke type.

Besides absorbing a higher-sink-rate landing the new undercarriage, together with its fatter tyres, would enable the C-130J to "swallow" bumps and therefore taxi faster over rough surfaces. This was found to be essential at Khe Sanh, where taxiing transport aircraft were vulnerable to artillery, mortar and rocket fire besides the more usual small-arms threat.

Engine for the C-130J would be the Allison

Externally similar to the C-130E, the H features improved flight-control, navigation and air-conditioning systems, and a beefed-up wing centre section.

The LC-130R version of the C-130H is probably the largest ski-equipped aircraft in the world. Six examples are operated by the US Navy's Antarctic support unit.

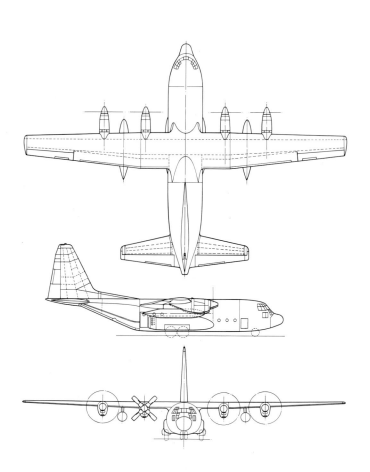

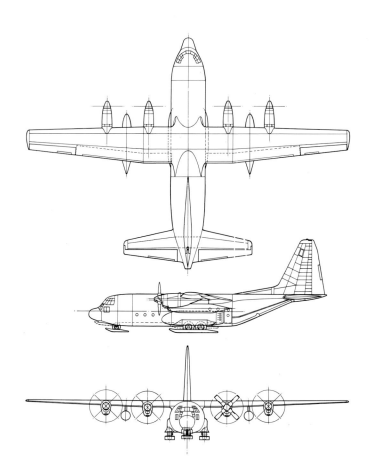

T56-A-15 rated at 4,910 shp. To absorb the extra power the reduction gearbox would be modified to maintain a propeller speed of 1,105 rpm. The increase in propeller speed would give better short take-off and landing (Stol) characteristics, but would incur an efficiency penalty of 2.5 per cent in the cruise.

The throttle quadrant would be fitted with a vernier stop to enable reverse thrust to be selected at higher power levels. The stop would be pre-positioned by the pilot from data derived from an airfield altitude/temperature compensation chart. This, combined with a higher propeller blade angle-change rate, would give the C-130J 30 per cent more reverse thrust than the C-130E.

Helping the pilot to make an accurate Stol approach would be a new instrument, the Speed Command of Altitude and Thrust (SCAT). The SCAT would give the pilot the means to maintain optimum lift for approach go-around and angle-of-attack data, each providing anticipatory data for the other. Also new would be the Inertial-Lead Vertical Speed Indicator, replacing the conventional rate-of-climb/descent indicator. Driven barometrically, the IVSI would also have data inputs from a vertical accelerometer to provide anticipation and improve the response rate. Purely barometrically driven instruments tend to lag.

A number of changes based on wind tunnel tests were recommended to improve the handling at the low speeds necessary for good Stol performance. The C-130J would have a 40 per cent increase in rudder chord and a larger dorsal fillet in front of the fin. A fully powered rudder with a fail-safe yaw-stability augmentor would reduce the minimum control speed to 73 kt from the 92 kt of the C-130E. The sideslip angle possible before the fin stalled would increase from the 18° of the C-130E to 28°. Roll control would be improved by a 30 per cent increase in aileron chord, while pitch control would benefit from an additional 5° of elevator-down deflection.

Approach altitude and landing speed would be improved by new hinged trailing-edge flaps which would be equivalent to a 50°-down deflection of the existing flaps. The C-130J would have take-off and landing rolls up to 50 per cent shorter than those of the C-130E.

To aid survivability some payload was to be traded off for armour. On the flightdeck the crew would wear flak suits plus chest armour and be seated in armoured seats. Wherever feasible, armoured material would be used for primary flightdeck structure.

The fuel system would also be armoured. The external tanks – the most vulnerable on the C-130 – would be removed before an assault flight and refitted for normal transit flights. The inboard main tanks would be surrounded by a self-sealing blanket and both inboard and outboard tanks would have an instantaneously acting fire and explosion-suppression system. Auxiliary fuel tanks would be purged of vapour by high-pressure air bled in from wing leading-edge intakes.

The fatigue life of the wing was to be improved by a stronger lower structure and the fitting of a rapid fuel-transfer pump. In the cruise fuel would be in outboard wing tanks to give bending relief, but it would be transferred rapidly inboard for the landing, improving handling at low speed and on the ground, besides being in the better-protected inboard tanks.

The US Air Force regarded the C-130J with great interest. In Vietnam many Hercules were being damaged by small-arms fire and shrapnel while operating from "hot" strips such as Pleiku, An Loc and Khe Sanh.

But the service was already looking ahead at a C-130 replacement. Requests for proposals for an Advanced Medium Stol Transport were going out. Lockheed incorporated many of the C-130J's features in its submission, the C-130SS (Stretched Stol). This Hercules variant would have had a longer fuselage to accommodate 20 more combat-equipped troops. The main differences between the C-130J and the C-130SS were that the AMST proposal would have massive triple-slotted wing trailing-edge flaps and roll-control enhancement at low speed by spoilers on the wing.

Boeing and McDonnell Douglas also entered the arena with two new designs, the YC-14 and YC-15. The twin-turbofan Boeing YC-14 and the four-turbofan McDonnell Douglas YC-15 were both superb designs, incorporating the latest in aerodynamic principles. Both were selected to be built for evaluation. Bemused as ever by new technology, the US Government did not fund the C-130SS. This was unfortunate for the US Air Force because both the new types proved too expensive, and the AMST programme eventually ran out of steam. The US Air Force was left wondering how many C-130SS it could have had in service for the funds spent developing the YC-14 and YC-15.

Advanced Hercules that never made it. **Below** C-130WBS (wide-body Stol) would have been wider, taller and longer than the standard Hercules. **Bottom** The C-130VLS proposal featured a T-tail and wider aft ramp. (Lockheed)

Rocket-assisted take-off gear in action as an LC-130R of the US Navy's UXE-6 lifts off from its Antarctic runway. Note the semi-official *Penguin Express* badge above the crew door.

Hercules variants

Think of a job, and the chances are that Lockheed has pro-posed a sub-model of the C-130 to do it, if that particular variant is not already in service somewhere. With a long production run behind it, the Hercules is a comparatively cheap aircraft to buy and a reliable and economical platform on which to base special-role equipment. A good range or endurance, inherent ruggedness, and load-carrying ability are qualities that are envied by salesmen of lesser aircraft.

By fitting plug-in modules the emergent nation can use the cost-effective C-130 instead of buying several different types. A firefighter? Yes, but not every day. Perhaps your country needs to keep an eye on the illegal fishing of young mackerel at a particular time of year. A quick module change and the Hercules can do it. When the fish stop running and the trees stop burning the Hercules can carry bulky equipment into the desert for your oil exploration programme, take your national team to the Olympic Games, drop paratroops, or seed clouds to fight drought. That is why the Hercules sells, why there are so many variants.

If the operator does not suffer from a lack of funds, as do some Third World countries, then he can have mission-dedicated variants instead of plug-in modules. The permutations appear to be endless, but listed below are the main sub-types and some options which did not leave the drawing board.

This Royal Saudi Air Force Hercules is equipped as a hospital capable of the most delicate open-heart surgery. The aircraft frequently accompanied the late King Khaled, who suffered heart trouble.

AC-130A Sixteen gunships converted from C-130s and JC-130As.

C-130A-II Ten C-130As modified for electronic intelligence-gathering.

DC-130A Seven aircraft modified to carry, launch and direct reconnaissance drones such as the Teledyne Ryan AQM-34/BQM-34 Firebee series. This variant was originally designated GC-130.

A standard C-130H Hercules, *City of Marietta* is shown in the now widespread USAF "European 1" camouflage scheme, and is flown by an Air Force Reserve crew, as indicated by the AFRes fin marking. The USAF's search for a C-130 replacement is now centred on the McDonnell Douglas C-17 proposal, having been through a stage in the mid-1970s when the ultra-Stol McDonnell Douglas YC-15 and Boeing YC-14 were both evaluated and then later dropped. The fact remains that the only feasible Hercules replacement (taking into account the cost of research and development) is another Hercules, and the type will probably continue in production until at least 1990 and very likely longer

C-130H leading data

Mission Tactical transport

Powerplant Four Allison T56-A-15 turboprops flat-rated to 4,508 ehp

Armament None

Avionics Dual HF, VHF and UHF communications, dual VHF nav, single UHF nav, CMA771 Omega nav, LTN-72 INS, dual DF206 DME, radar altimeter, RDF-1 weather radar, Tacan, autopilot, ground-proximity warning system, stationkeeping equipment

Dimensions
Wing span 132 ft 7 in (40.41 m)
Length overall 97 ft 9 in (34.37 m)
Height overall 38.ft 3 in (11.66 m)
Wing area 1,745 ft² (162.12 m²)

Weights
Empty 76,469 lb (34,686 kg)
Max take-off (overload) 175,000 lb (79,380 kg)
Max payload 42,673 lb (19,356 kg)

Performance
Maximum speed 325 kt
Service ceiling 33,000 ft (at 130,000 lb AUW)
Range with max payload 2,046 nm (7,876 km)

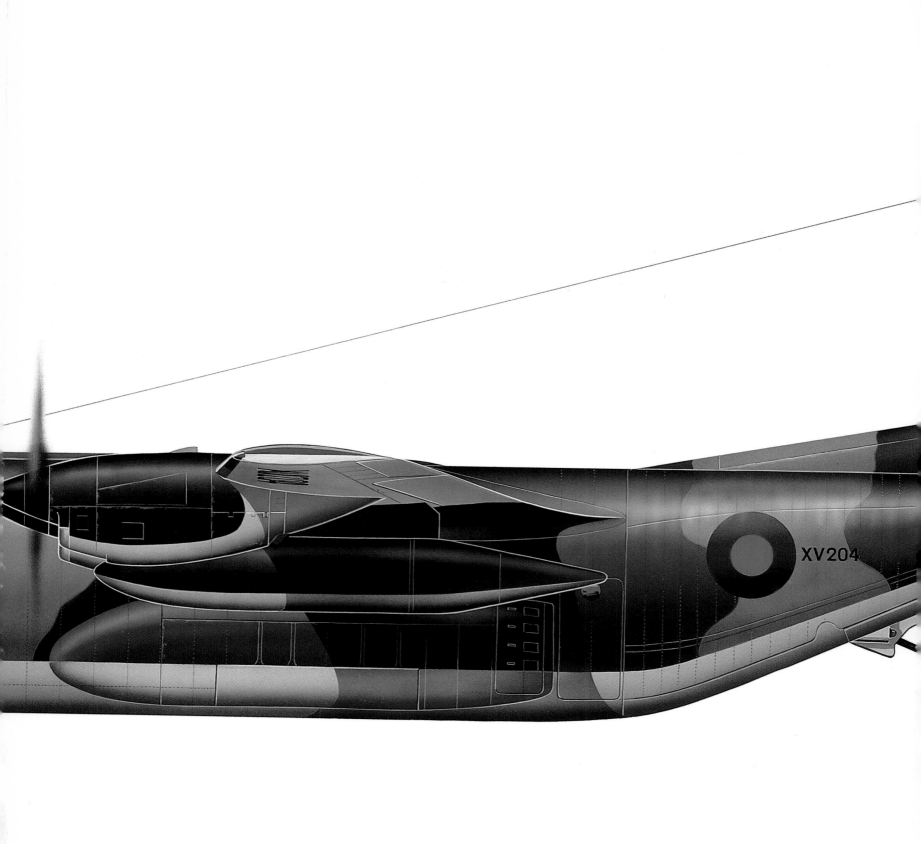

ROYAL AIR FORCE

204

James Goulding.

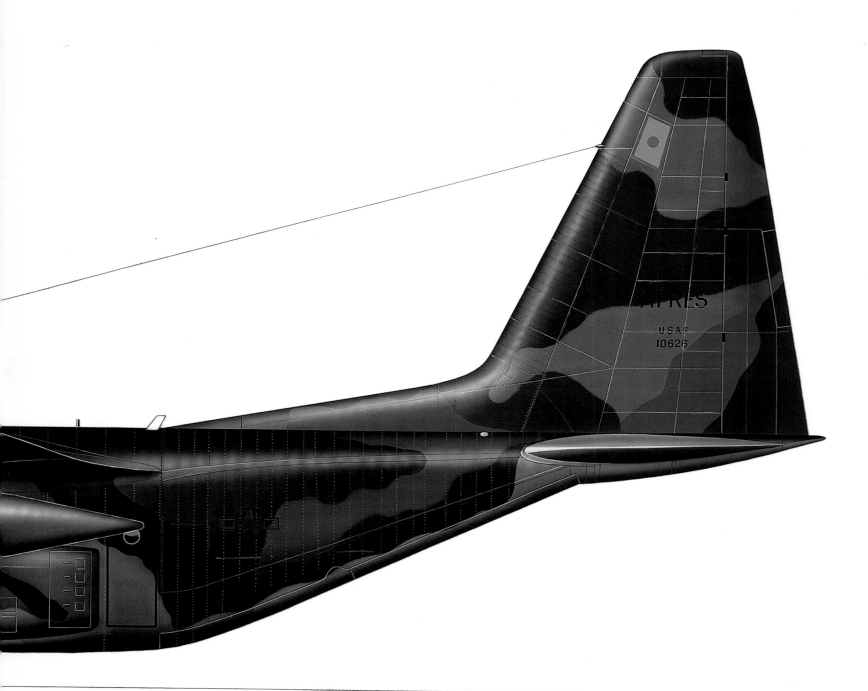

James Goulding

Above A US Air Force C-130H kicks up the dust on Pope AFB's sand strip. The low-pressure tyres and reverse thrust make off-runway operations remarkably simple.

Below This ski-and-rocket-fitted C-130D is operated by the New York Air National Guard. Note the four windows aft of the crew entry door, three-blade propellers and small outboard wing tanks, which denote conversion from a C-130A. (Lockheed)

During the Falklands War it soon became apparent that the RAF's fleet of Victor tankers could not cope with the heavy workload created by operations from and to Ascension Island. In little over three weeks from conception to first flight, Marshall of Cambridge converted the first of four standard Hercules to tanker/receiver configuration. Another 16 Hercs were converted to receiver-only standard. The tanker modification entails fitting a 500 gal/min-capable Mk 17 hose-drum unit in the tail ramp, a drogue deployment box externally, and two 1,800 gal long-range tanks internally. Although the tanker Hercules can refuel anything in the RAF inventory (between 180 kt and 300 kt, up to 25,000 ft), the aircraft are usually based at Port Stanley in support of the Phantoms, Harriers, Nimrods and other Hercules based there. The receiver aircraft depicted here is a Tornado GR.1 of 617 Sqn.

C-130K Hercules C.1(K) leading data

Mission In-flight refuelling

Powerplant Four Allison T56-A-15 turboprops, flat-rated to 4,508 ehp

Armament None

Avionics Standard fit of HF/VHF/UHF radios, VOR/DME, Tacan and RDR-1F radar, plus Omega global navigation and flight-refuelling control panels fitted at navigator's station. Floodlights illuminate aircraft underside for night refuelling, and two sets of retractable refuelling "traffic lights" are mounted on ramp

Dimensions
Wing span 132 ft 7 in (40.41 m)
Length overall 97 ft 9 in (34.37 m)
Height overall 38 ft 3 in (11.66 m)
Wing area 1,745 ft² (162.12 m²)

Performance
Maximum speed 325 kt
Service ceiling 33,000 ft (25,000 ft refuelling)
Total fuel capacity 28,000 lb

Above The single C-130H operated by the Gabon Air Force.

Below One of several recent C-130H recipients is the Algerian Air Force. The aircraft are said to have been supplied by a thankful US Government in return for Algeria's help in negotiations to release the hostages from the US embassy in Tehran. (Lockheed)

GC-130A Original DC-130A designation, but applied to one grounded C-130A used for instruction of maintenance personnel.

JC-130A Missile-tracking Hercules used to observe launches from Cape Canaveral, converted from 16 C-130As. Six later modified to AC-130A configuration.

NC-130A Used as test vehicles, the five NC-130s were later converted back to standard C-130As.

RC-130A Aerial survey and photographic mapping aircraft. Sixteen built, later modified to C-130A.

TC-130A Prototype crew trainer, modified to RC-130A.

C-130B II Elint version of B model, later called RC-130B. Thirteen conversions, which eventually reverted to transport duties.

C-130BL Original designation for four ski-equipped C-130Bs for US Navy use in Antarctica. Redesignated UV-1L then LC-130F.

HC-130B Twelve search and rescue variants for US Coast Guard. Original designation was R8V-1G.

Among the smartest Hercules are the US Coast Guard HC-130s. This aircraft is patrolling the Florida coastline. "We get plenty of trade from idiots in cabin cruisers using a page from a school atlas to try and navigate to Bermuda and the like," one coastguardsman told the author.

JC-130B Fourteen built with nose forks and inboard winch for airborne recovery of film capsules from reconnaissance satellites.

KC-130B Two C-130Bs modified as tankers for Indonesian Air Force.

NC-130B Boundary-layer control test vehicle with two Allison J56 turbojets mounted on outboard pylons.

RC-130B See C-130B II.

SC-130B Interim designation of HC-130B.

VC-130B Interim VIP transport modification of one JC-130B, subsequently returned to C-130B standard.

WC-130B Weather reconnaissance platform, 14 aircraft.

C-130C Not built, proposed BLC Stol model.

C-130D C-130A modified with ski undercarriage, 12 aircraft for US Navy.

AC-130E Eleven gunship modifications under Pave Spectre programme, ten survivors upgraded to AC-130H standard.

DC-130E Seven drone launchers/directors.

The EC-130E is distinguished by three extremely large blade aerials – one dorsal and two underwing – and pod and tail-mounted housings for trailing aerials.

EC-130E Airborne battlefield command post designation for eight aircraft previously known as C-130E II and re-engined later to become EC-130H.

HC-130E Nineteen aircraft with Fulton recovery nose fork. Later changed from combat rescue role to special operations and modified with FLIR and terrain-following radar plus electronic countermeasures and passive self-defence equipment in Combat Talon programme, redesignated MC-130E.

JC-130E One aircraft, tested as missile tracker.

MC-130E Combat Talon, see HC-130E.

NC-130E Combat Talon test aircraft.

WC-130E Weather reconnaissance.

C-130F US Navy version of C-130B. Seven aircraft originally designated GV-1U.

KC-130F US Marine Corps tanker, 46 built.

LC-130F Post-1962 designation for US Navy C-130BL/UV-1L.

C-130G US Navy version of C-130E, four built.

EC-130G Four C-130Gs modified with very-low-frequency communications to relay fire-control messages between the Pentagon and submerged ballistic missile submarines in TACAMO (Take Charge and Move Out) programme. Superseded by EC-130Q.

C-130H(CT) Fifteen MC-130E with updated mission equipment and T56-A-15 engines.

C-130H(MP) Maritime patrol variant.

C-130H(S) Stretched C-130H, equivalent of RAF Hercules C.3 and civil L-100-30. Redesignated C-130H-30.

AC-130H Upgunned, upgraded AC-130E with T56-A-15 engines and in-flight refuelling capability.

DC-130H Prototype heavyweight drone launcher/controller, not proceeded with.

EC-130E Re-engined with T56-A-15.

HC-130H Search and rescue aircraft, 43 built, all with Fulton recovery nose and roof-mounted Cook Tracker radar.

In-flight refuelling is another string to the Hercules bow. This US Marine Corps KC-130F is topping up a pair of F-4 Phantoms.

KC-130H Tanker version of C-130H for overseas sales.

JHC-130H Aerial satellite-pod recovery aircraft, the two JHC-130Hs were modified from HC-130Hs. Later redesignated NC-130H.

VC-130H Two VIP transports for Royal Family of Saudi Arabia.

The elaborate HC-130H conversion typifies the lengths to which the US services will go to rescue downed aircrew.

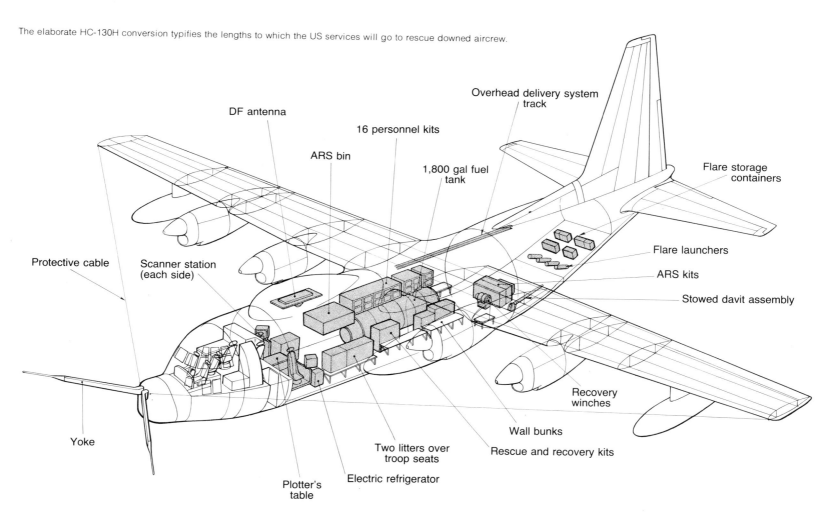

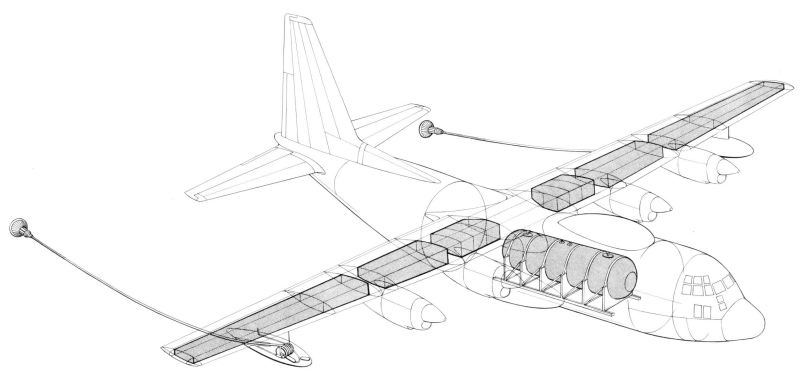

Layout of the fuel system aboard the KC-130H export tanker. A number of British C-130Ks have also been modified as tankers, fitted with a single hose-drum unit deploying through the cargo ramp. These aircraft are designated C.1(K) by the RAF.

WC-130H Weather reconnaissance, 15 aircraft modified from HC-130H.

C-130J Proposed assault-landing Stol Hercules.

C-130K C-130H with British avionics and equipment. Sixty-six delivered to Royal Air Force as Hercules C.1. One modified as Hercules W.2, operated by Meteorological Flight of Royal Aircraft Establishment. Thirty stretched to C-130H-30 standard as Hercules C.3. Four C.1s modified as tankers for the Falklands campaign, other C.1s and C.3s modified with inflight refuelling probe.

C-130L Designation not yet used.

C-130M Designation not yet used.

HC-130N Search and rescue aircraft with provision for increased internal fuel in cargo hold.

HC-130P Tanker/search and rescue variant.

EC-130Q Improved-avionics version of EC-130G, based on C-130H airframe.

KC-130R Tanker for US Marine Corps similar to KC-130H; 14 aircraft.

LC-130R Ski-undercarriage version of C-130H; six for US Navy Antarctic resupply mission.

RC-130S Battlefield Illumination Airborne System with 28 lights arranged in pods on fuselage sides. Two RC-130S were modified from JC-130As for use in Vietnam.

This WC-130H was originally a rescue and recovery HC-130H. The chisel-shaped nose radome was designed to accommodate the nose yoke while the dorsal radome contained an ultra-sensitive VHF/UHF direction-finder known as a Cook Tracker.

LC-130Rs are equipped with up to eight jettisonable rocket-assisted take-off (RATO) bottles to help get off packed snow runways at heavy weight.

Record-breaker: the DC-130H

The Hercules holds several world records for endurance and point-to-point speeds. Other records include those for largest aircraft to take off and land on an aircraft carrier, the world's heaviest low-altitude cargo extraction (25 tons dropped from 10 ft), the longest flight by a commercial aircraft (the L-100 maiden flight of 25 hr 1 min), and distance records for nonstop, non-refuelled turboprop flight (8,790 statute miles, from Taiwan to Scott AFB, Illinois). With the possible exception of the L-100 first flight, which was a public relations extravaganza, all of the record-breaking epics have proved a valid operational concept.

But discard any visions of a bored Lockheed executive thumbing through the *Guinness Book of Records* looking for targets. Record-breaking is a spin-off – albeit a valuable one for the C-130 sales team – of hard work from the design and product-engineering departments striving to meet new, tougher operational goals. An example was the development of the sole DC-130H, converted from an HC-130H.

The "A" and "E" models of the DC-130 had been in service with the US Air Force and US Navy for some time. The DCs, or "Dumbos", were used to launch various types of remotely piloted vehicles. These drones were used extensively in Vietnam to photograph "hot" or heavily defended targets in North Vietnam, acting as decoys to pinpoint new SAM sites, or simply flying around on electronic intelligence-gathering missions, "listening" to and recording enemy radio and radar transmissions. The RPVs were launched from the DC-130 mother ship and flown to the target and back by specialists aboard the DC-130.

As the missions became tougher the RPVs carried more systems to cope with defences. Inevitably, the RPVs grew heavier and more complex until a new launch/director aircraft, able to cope with the increased weight and complexity, was needed. The H model could, with modification, carry more weight than the "Es" and "As". The Lockheed Aircraft Service Company based at Ontario, California, was awarded a $5.5 million US Air Force contract to build a third-generation RPV mother-ship demonstrator.

The US Air Force specification called for the parent aircraft to carry four RPVs weighing up to 10,000 lb each, drop them at 15 sec intervals, and guide them simultaneously. The modifications to convert a C-130H into a DC-130H included reinforcing the wing, installing more powerful electrical generators, extending the nose to accommodate tracking and telemetry antennae, changing the cargo hold into a control centre with large windows to permit observation of the RPVs before launch, fitting Loran radar area-navigation equipment, and installing the plumbing and wiring for the four underwing RPV pylons.

It was required that the wings should not only support a 40,000 lb dead weight, but that they should absorb the stress of sudden deflection loads as the payload was released. The wing was made stiffer and stronger by adding reinforcing straps to the main spar and to the ribs, both top and bottom, along their entire lengths.

The pylons were "wet", ie the RPV's tanks could be topped up in flight from the DC-130. This allowed the RPV engines to be used for boosting take-offs from hot, high or humid airfields. Provision had to be made for the pylons to carry not only the drones in service, but also those still on the drawing board. Moreover, the pylons were to have internal fire extinguishers for themselves and for the RPVs, and had to be interchangeable between all four wing stations. As if that were not enough, provision had to be made for the standard Hercules long-range tanks to be reinstalled for extended missions. On the electrical side, the generators were upgraded from 40 kVA to 60 kVA and all of the contactors, main wiring, and bus-bars were beefed up to take the extra load.

Internally the aircraft was fitted with a new operations compartment with accommodation for two launch control officers, a remote control officer, a weapon control officer (some RPVs were armed with TV-guided bombs and missiles), and a radar technician. Observers and/or trainees could also be carried. Lighting, air conditioning and sound-proofing of the enclosed operations compartment were improved over the standard of earlier DC-130 models.

The Loran navigation system of the DC-130H was continuously locked into a computer-controlled plotter in the operations compartment, thus giving a continuous reading of the DC-130's position. The telemetry in the DC-130's nose plotted each RPV's position and the RPV fed back, via a digital data link, its own height, course and airspeed. Thus the flight controller had a constant readout of each RPV's position in relation to the ground.

Launch of the RPVs was conducted from two stations in the rear of the compartment, the launch consoles being substantially redesigned. On the DC-130H the launch controllers are able to check each RPV's serviceability simultaneously and then "ripple-launch" them at 15 sec intervals.

Built-in safety factors included over-ride circuitry in the cockpit with an emergency jettison switch and provision to release the RPV's recovery parachute should it accidentally deploy before release from the mother ship. Also in the cockpit were fire warning lights for the RPVs and the pylons, and the manually activated extinguisher circuits for use should the automatic devices fail. The flight engineer could also preset a rapid fuel transfer sequence to offset roll-trim changes during asymmetric launches.

The wing strengthening was tested on the ground at Ontario by the simultaneous drop of four 10,000 lb weights. Everything performed as predicted and nothing fell off the aircraft that wasn't meant to do so. Following this test the DC-130H was test-flown from Edwards AFB with four specially built masses of 10,000 lb, each simulating one of the new RPVs. The 16 flight tests from Edwards went well, and in August 1977 the sole DC-130H was assigned to Hill AFB for operational evaluation.

Everything was going well, but then the US Air Force abandoned its RPV philosophy and development was stopped. The Air Force's reasoning has never been adequately explained. Perhaps advances in optical and synthetic

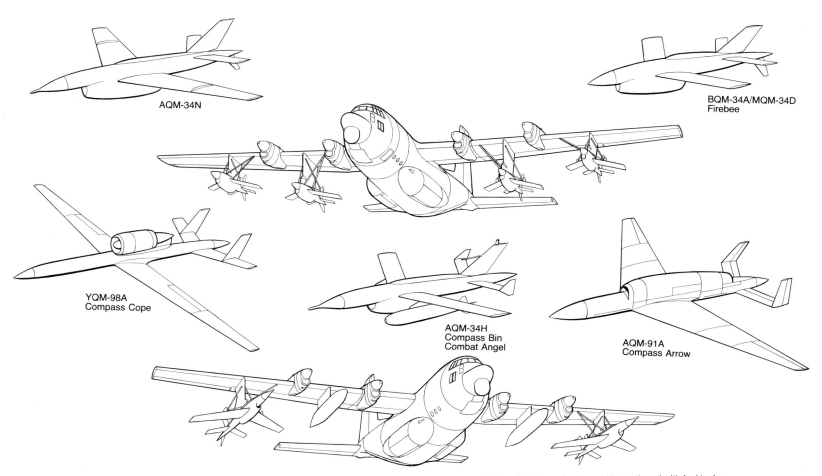

AQM-34N

BQM-34A/MQM-34D
Firebee

YQM-98A
Compass Cope

AQM-34H
Compass Bin
Combat Angel

AQM-91A
Compass Arrow

The drone-control Hercules have carried a remarkable number and variety of RPVs over the years. For long-range missions the inboard pair could be replaced with fuel tanks.

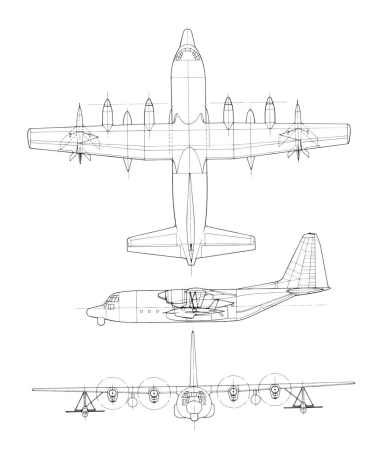

Above DC-130A, the original drone-carrying variant.

Above left The sole DC-130H setting an unofficial world record by lifting four underwing bodies totalling 44,510 lb.

Left DC-130A drone-controller carrying Teledyne Ryan Model 147 RPV.   (Teledyne Ryan)

imagery available from satellite reconnaissance rendered the RPVs unnecessary. Whatever the reason, the US Air Force was left with the most advanced drone director ever built, and Lockheed was left a world record for consolation, instead of a production contract.

Stanleyville rescue

The Hercules has taken part in many campaigns as well as one-off missions such as the Entebbe rescue. In some wars it has served with both sides, the most recent example being the short but vicious conflict between Argentina and Great Britain in 1982. Its primary role of transporting troops and their equipment has never really stolen the headlines, but without the Hercules and its crews working day and night, often in appalling conditions, many soldiers of many nations would not be alive today.

The C-130 had its first whiff of cordite at Stanleyville in the Belgian Congo in 1964. As this book was written the last C-130 to fly into a combat zone was an Argentinian Air Force C-130 sneaking into Port Stanley the night before Argentinian troops surrendered the Falkland Islands.

In the Congo, the rebel "Simbas" had taken 1,600 foreign civilians hostage at Stanleyville. The hostages were mainly white Europeans, with a sprinkling of American consular staff and a few hundred Asians. In outlying districts foreign missionaries, farmers and engineers were rounded up. Some were killed, a great many were tortured, and some – the lucky ones – were sent to Stanleyville or the township of Paulis to the north. The rebels forced the Belgian Consul to tell the USA and Belgium that the foreign nationals would be freed only if the two countries stopped supporting the Congo's legitimate government under Premier Tshombe.

Newly elected American President Lyndon Johnson and Belgian Prime Minister Paul Spaak agreed to mount a joint rescue. Operation Dragon Rouge would use US Air Force C-130Es based at Evreux, France, to transport the Belgian 1st Parachute Battalion to Stanleyville. The paras would arrive in two waves. First, 320 of them would parachute in and secure the airfield. This would allow the second wave of 125 paras and their vehicles to be landed. Leaving a small contingent to protect the airfield, the paras would then move into Stanleyville to rescue the hostages and bring them back through a secure lane to the airfield for evacuation. With the Congo government's approval, the operation was to be mounted from Kamina in the southern Congo.

At Evreux on Sunday 15 November Col Gradwell of the 322nd Air Division was tasked with setting up 12 C-130Es to be ready to leave on the following Tuesday. Half of his E-model aircraft were scattered throughout Europe on routine jobs. Aircraft captains received signals to return to base immediately. Although Gradwell had a squadron of C-130s based on temporary rotation duty at Evreux, he had to have the "E" models because the "As" couldn't cope with the range and payload combination.

On the Tuesday morning 12 C-130Es left Evreux under sealed orders. Calling first at Kleine Brogel in Belgium

A Hercules drops heavy equipment in support of a paratroop assault.

to pick up the paratroopers, they then headed out over France and Spain to Ascension Island in the South Atlantic, which was reached on the Wednesday. Meanwhile, nine Douglas C-124 Globemasters flew to the Congo with backup equipment for the Hercs.

After a day to relax and sleep the Belgian paras, who had never jumped from C-130s before, boarded the Hercs for a series of practice jumps. While the Belgians and Americans were getting to know one another's operating methods two other Hercules arrived at Leopoldville carrying a portable HF radio station. This field rig would be set up at Kamina to enable the joint force to maintain contact with Brussels and Washington.

The situation in Stanleyville was worsening, with the rebels threatening to execute the hostages unless the US Government agreed to "negotiate". Playing for time, the US State Department agreed that negotiations – on what subject was not clear – would start the following Monday, 23 November. At the same time the 12 C-130s were instructed to position at Kamina. They arrived early on Sunday morning after a 2,500-mile flight from Ascension. One of the pre-positioned Hercules, relieved of its load of radio and generator equipment, was now available to the strike force as a spare aircraft. The other Hercules was to remain at Kamina as the radio link and command post.

Meanwhile, President Jomo Kenyatta of Kenya attempted to mediate between the rebels and the Western powers. The rebel's demand was simple, if naïve. Unless the USA and Belgium stopped Tshombe's army and mercenaries from intervening in Simba activities, the hostages would die. The USA said that the proposals were blackmail and contravened international law. The Pentagon immediately flashed a signal to Kamina – the mission was on.

Gradwell and the Belgian commander, Col Laurent, received the "go" signal at 2200 on Monday 23 November. The aircraft and paras, already in a high state of readiness, took off at 10 sec intervals starting at 0245 hr on Tuesday morning.

Arriving over Stanleyville Airport at dawn, the first wave of five C-130s ran in at 700 ft and 125 kt. Despite ground fire the Americans maintained their line and dropped the 320 Belgians on to the grass next to the runway. On a second run the five Hercs dropped the Belgians' heavier equipment, machine guns, mortars and anti-tank rockets. Four of the Hercs then departed to a holding point while the lead ship set up an orbit at 2,000 ft to clear in the next seven C-130s. The Belgians were by now all safely down and in 40 min had cleared the Simbas holding the airport buildings and tower and had removed obstructions from the runway.

The second wave of seven aircraft set down rapidly, bringing in more paras and their vehicles for the dash into Stanleyville, two miles away.

Taking no chances on their way into the town, the paras poured barrages of automatic fire into the surrounding undergrowth, killing a few would-be snipers in the process. Conducting a house-to-house search, the Belgians started to collect hostages held in their own homes and take them to the airport. Some 300 white hostages held in the town centre were not so lucky. The Simbas had herded them outside and, after arguing between themselves, started shooting their captives. The hostages scattered and ran for cover, but 22 fell dead or dying.

As the Simbas prepared to kill the wounded, the Belgian paras came upon the scene and quickly despatched the rebels. The freed hostages and other whites who had been in hiding were now being hurried back to the airport, where the last of the second wave was approaching through the Simba ground fire. Several C-130s were hit on their way in and out of Stanleyville, but none of the strikes were serious.

Gradwell's aircraft, still circling at 2,000 ft, was hit several times.

Down on the airfield the Hercules were waiting for the hostages with engines running. Loading as many people as possible, their crews then taxied fast to minimize exposure to ground fire from Simbas who were again infiltrating the airfield. Maximum-performance take-offs were the order of the day, the aircraft climbing steeply and then flying flat out for Kamina to offload the wounded, who were now being tended by medical staff.

Other aircraft were now inbound to Stanleyville to help with the evacuation, and Congolese government forces had reached the outskirts to link with the paras. Two days later Dragon Noir, a similar mission mounted to Paulis, north of Stanleyville, rescued another 355 hostages. In four days the Hercules was instrumental in saving nearly 2,000 people from gruesome deaths at the hands of the Simbas.

Khe Sanh mortar magnet

Located 15 miles south of the demilitarized zone (DMZ) and some six miles east of South Vietnam's border with Laos, Khe Sanh straddled the east–west highway, Route 9. Two miles north was Khe Sanh Combat Base. Set up by the US Army Special Forces in 1962, the base had been handed over to the US Marine Corps and expanded slightly in January 1967.

Built on a plateau, Khe Sanh was the main base, with outposts of various sizes on top of the neighbouring hills. From Khe Sanh US Marines and the Army of the Republic of Vietnam, known as Arvins, launched patrols into the

Hercules taxis at speed through the shot and shell raining down on the besieged Marine Corps bastion at Khe Sanh.

(Lockheed)

surrounding countryside, keeping "Charlie" on the hop and disrupting his lines of supply.

Because of the hilltop location, ground supply routes to the Khe Sanh base were vulnerable, so in 1967 a 1,500 ft runway of pierced-steel-planking (PSP) was constructed, with a small unloading area at the north-west end.

As the garrison was built up and the defences strengthened, C-130s flew in to Khe Sanh for the first time, hauling supplies from Tan San Nhut. But it was the rainy season and the PSP runway, laid on clay, could not stand the pounding of the maximum-performance landings needed to get C-130s into the short strip. Supply continued using the C-7 Caribou, but the smaller aircraft could not fly in the bulldozers, graders and tons of PSP needed to repair and lengthen the runway. Some of the equipment was parachuted in by C-130s, but it was too risky to drop the heavier equipment from normal altitudes. The base was small, and the margin of error with winds swirling around the plateau could easily result in heavy loads dropping into the camp area.

The answer was LAPES, the Low-Altitude Parachute Extraction System. Wheels and flaps down, the C-130s approached at about 130–140 kt, skimming over the runway at between six and ten feet. As the aircraft crossed the perimeter, ramp down and nose up, the pilot flashed a light signal to the loadmaster in the cargo hold, who pulled a cord to release a small drogue or pilot parachute on the load pallet. This streamed from the aircraft and pulled out the main chute. As the main parachute filled it pulled the load from the C-130's tail ramp. The load then dropped the few feet to the runway, the impact being absorbed by the specially cushioned pallet. As the Hercules climbed away into the circuit for another drop, the load's main parachutes slowed the pallet down, acting purely as a brake. The LAPES drops were successful, and the US Navy's Seabees extended Khe Sanh's runway to 3,900 ft. Within a few months it became the outpost's lifeline.

In December 1967 the North Vietnamese Army joined the Vietcong in the area around Khe Sanh. By early January the Marines estimated that two NVA divisions of 10,000 men each were positioned in the hills just north of the base. The battle started on 21 January with attacks on outposts, and the 3,500 US Marines settled into their defensive positions, ready for a fight and confident that they had adequate supplies of ammunition.

The situation changed on the first day, when North Vietnamese artillery set fire to Khe Sanh's main munitions dump. A series of explosions ripped through the ammunition, destroying 1,340 tons within minutes, and the barrage also holed the runway in several places. The Marines' serious but manageable situation had deteriorated to the point where they were now in danger of being overwhelmed through lack of ammunition.

The Seabees again repaired the runway, this time under fire from artillery and mortars in the surrounding hills. But they could only repair enough runway to take the smaller C-123 Providers; the Hercules could still not get in. Flying day and night from Da Nang and landing in the dark by the light of parachute flares, the Providers brought 116 tons of ammunition into Khe Sanh in 48 hr. However, the Marines were using it as fast as it was delivered, fending off repeated mass assaults by the NVA. To build up a reserve stock the larger C-130 was needed. Again LAPES deliveries provided materials, and this time Seabees managed to repair enough runway to allow the C-130s to get in.

By now the NVA had set up anti-aircraft artillery (AAA) on the approaches to Khe Sanh's tiny runway. The slow piston-engined Providers were vulnerable, and one was hit on the approach, crashing with the loss of 48 lives. The faster C-130s were not such easy targets in the air, but they were just as vulnerable while unloading on the ground. A US Marine Corps KC-130F carrying bladders of helicopter fuel was hit as it flew in on 11 February. The fuel ignited and the Herc slammed on to the runway in a ball of fire. The two pilots survived, but the other six crew members perished.

Marine Warrant Officer Henry Wildfang, an old *and* bold pilot with 15,000 hr and four Distinguished Flying Crosses from service in Korea and Vietnam, earned his fifth DFC at Khe Sanh. When his KC-130 was hit on the approach by AAA while carrying a load of fuel, Wildfang managed to get the blazing aircraft down in one piece, saving his crew, and then taxied the burning Hercules off the runway to allow another to land before he closed down the engines and got out.

The North Vietnamese mortar crews were notoriously accurate, so the crews unloaded the C-130s in record time. Sometimes the cargo pallets would be unlocked and shoved down the ramp on the inbuilt roller conveyors even as the aircraft was taxiing through the dispersal loop off the runway. The Marines defending Khe Sanh looked upon the C-130s as a mixed blessing. The Hercs brought in the food and ammunition needed for survival and flew out the wounded for treatment, but while they were on the ground they attracted so much fire that the Marines dubbed them "Mortar Magnets".

Even in a 3 min "running" turnround the C-130s spent too long on the ground. The longer landing run of the C-130, compared with those of the smaller C-7s and C-123s, meant that the Hercules had to taxi further. Although few aircraft were totally destroyed by ground fire, the maintenance crews were hard-pressed to repair the shrapnel damage. Some aircraft arrived back at base with more than 200 holes in them. In mid-February it was decided that the Hercules were too valuable to risk on the ground at Khe Sanh. Moreover, the full load capability of the C-130 could not be realized while operating on to Khe Sanh's short PSP runway, which again was beginning to suffer from the Hercules' pounding.

So the C-130s returned to parachute dropping. A drop zone (DZ) was established to the west of the runway, but normal parachute delivery had two disadvantages. First, the accuracy had to be spot-on, otherwise the enemy received the supplies. Secondly, the Marines were exposed to enemy fire as they retrieved the containers. The US Air Force returned to LAPES as its main delivery mode. As before, the C-130s came under ground fire on the approach, but each aircraft was followed by a forward air controller in a light aircraft who would spot and pinpoint the enemy AAA sites with smoke rockets. The FAC would then bring in an air or artillery strike to remove the threat. The area around Khe Sanh was also regularly pounded by B-52 "Arc Light" strikes, mounted from Guam.

Even with LAPES accurate delivery remained a problem. Some loads were dropped from slightly too high and bounced along, disintegrating and ruining the PSP runway in the process. Also the C-130s had to fly very close to a wrecked C-123, which was an additional safety hazard. On 2 March a LAPES-drop error resulted in a heavy cargo pallet hitting a gun position, killing one Marine and injuring others.

To resolve the problems of accuracy and the growing shortage of parachutes the C-130 crews tried a modified LAPES. An arrester cable was strung across the runway at a convenient point. Flying low, the Hercules trailed a grappling hook from the load. The hook engaged the cable, yanked out the load and brought it to a halt exactly where it was needed. The cable position was changed regularly to avoid excess wear on one part of the runway.

With the problem solved, the flights continued. When the Vietnamese abandoned the seige in mid-April 1968, the C-130s had made 496 air supply drops, 57 LAPES and modified LAPES deliveries, and 273 landings at Khe Sanh. Together with the C-123 (179 landings, mainly in the early phases) and C-7 (only eight landings, early in the seige), the C-130 delivered 12,400 tons of cargo. Without the C-130 Khe Sanh could have been as disastrous for the Americans as Dien Bien Phu proved for the French in the Fifties.

After the epic resupply of Khe Sanh, the Hercules bore the brunt of airlift operations in Vietnam on several occasions. As the North Vietnamese Army increased its overt operations in the early Seventies, the C-130 force was increasingly called upon to lift supplies, fuel and ammunition into beleaguered outposts.

Operating from Cam Ranh Bay and Tan Son Nhut, the Hercules supplied Pleiku when its road link with the coast was blocked by NVA forces at the An Khe Pass. The lift continued for 16 days from 16 April, 1972. Some aircraft, fitted with rubber fuel bladders in the cargo hold, delivered 41,500 gal on each trip.

Almost simultaneously with the ending of the Pleiku blockade, the road from Pleiku to Kontum was cut. The Hercules force switched destinations, delivering 24,000 gal of fuel to Kontum each day, interspersed with loads of hard goods: food, ammunition and medical supplies. As at Khe Sanh, the Hercules came under enemy fire – AAA and SA-7s on the approach and departure lanes and RPG-7 rockets and artillery, mortar and small-arms fire while on the ground. The rocket and mortar attacks eventually became so fierce that C-130 landings were made at night, while maintaining the level of supply.

When deliveries failed to keep pace with the increased expenditure of ammunition daylight resupply was resumed for a week, but night-only flights were then reintroduced. Republic of Vietnam Air Force (RVNAF) C-123 Providers helped out but, as at Khe Sanh, they were vulnerable while airborne and several were lost. A C-130 was hit by rockets and destroyed, and an AC-130 burned out on the ground after taking mortar hits. Several helicopters were also wrecked on the ground.

Tactics were changed to avoid the dangerous airline-type linear approach. The C-130s would arrive overhead the airfield at 10,000 ft, spiralling down from about 2,000 ft in a tight turn into a close-in visual circuit, switching on landing lights on the final turn.

At the same time AC-130s orbited at a slightly larger radius, watching for ground fire. The AC-130s would then use their laser designator to "sparkle" a target for F-4 Phantoms

Seconds to thump-down as a Hercules carries out a LAPES drop. Large-diameter parachutes and shock-absorbing pallets did the trick.

orbiting higher and further out, carrying laser-guided bombs.

Alternatively, an AC-130 could stand off and blast the enemy AAA sites with its 105 mm gun.

By 25 May the situation was so bad that the airfield at Kontum was about to be overrun. The last C-130s landed just before this to evacuate the US Air Force and RVNAF ground element. The final Herc out of Kontum lifted off as NVA infantry crossed the runway ahead. Further supplies would have to be parachuted to US and Arvin troops fighting a rearguard action in the city.

The C-130s used a new system called AWADS (All Weather Aerial Delivery System). AWADS was a computer carried on the aircraft and fed with the exact geographical co-ordinates of the drop zone, the height, course, speed and position of the aircraft, wind velocities, and the fall rate of the load. From this data AWADS would give the pilots "fly-to" information on the horizontal situation indicator. At the computed release point the load was dropped, and if all the variables had been accounted for the load would arrive on target.

The computer could be updated on the run-in by a ground-based radar beacon located on a known range and bearing from the load impact point. Alternatively, the Hercules' own radar could be used to update the system with echoes from salient features on the ground. Both methods were used at Kontum, a bridge and a river bend providing handy radar offsets to update the computer-calculated release point. All drops were made from 10,000 ft, out of range of the shoulder-launched SA-7 missile. The farthest drop from the target was only 300 m out.

Another new technique pioneered at Kontum was the formation AWADS drop. Using their formation-keeping radar beacons, C-130s flew in formation with an AWADS-equipped lead ship, releasing a few seconds after the leader. The beauty of AWADS was that, for the first time, the ground troops could rely on aerial resupply in any weather, night or day.

A third technique, called CDS (Container Delivery System), was used in the resupply by air of An Loc and Quan Loi. On a CDS drop the Hercules approached the target at 250 kt and as low as possible but not above 100 ft. On arriving at an Initial Point the aircraft was pulled up to 600 ft, slowing down to 130 kt to release 16 one-ton supply containers. As soon as the load was clear the aircraft dived into a low-level, high-speed exit from the area. The CDS run was supposed to reduce the length of time that the C-130 was exposed to enemy ground fire, but at An Loc four aircraft were hit over the drop zone and a fifth was shot down. At 130 kt and 600 ft an aircraft the size of a Hercules is harder to miss than hit. CDS was considered too risky and the idea was dropped.

The resupply effort continued, but at higher levels, beyond the range of the 37 mm AAA. The Ground Radar Aerial Delivery System (GRADS) was a reversal of AWADS. Instead of using its own radar, the aircraft was positioned by a ground radar operator. The parachutes on the loads stayed partly furled to minimize any wind-drift error until a barostatic trigger unfurled them a few hundred feet above the ground. Unfortunately the barostat triggers suf-

fered teething troubles and some loads impacted at terminal velocity. The Hercules forces returned to night CDS drops until the snag was sorted out. Eventually some 3,100 tons of supplies were GRADS-dropped into An Loc from 10,000 ft with better than 90 per cent accuracy. After nearly two months the North Vietnamese attack was broken. Again the Hercules had played a major role in the battle. Without it the city would have fallen.

Spectre!

9 November, 1967, was a bad day for Charlie. North Vietnamese Army (NVA) truck drivers had been driving a six-truck convoy along the Ho Chi Minh trail for several nights. Now, deep in Laos, the convoy was about halfway to its rendezvous with the Vietcong and NVA forces who would carry its load of armaments into South Vietnam. The night was black and cloudy, and the drivers' only problem was maintaining contact with a tiny, dull-red light under the tail-board of the truck in front.

Suddenly the sky rained streams of yellow, white and red fire. The solid stream of tracer "walked" through the jungle a few yards and the lead truck dissolved, literally disappearing in the firestorm. The following trucks skidded to an untidy halt in the mud, the drivers scrambling for cover as the last engine coughed and died. A drone of aircraft engines, previously covered by the trucks' noise, filtered through the tree canopy.

A few seconds later the fire cone again searched through the trees and hit the rear truck, which exploded in flames. The NVA drivers had seen similar scenes before from afar – but the noise! The gunfire sounded like the angry bellow of a bull. Without further ado the NVA drivers fled deep into the cool moisture of the jungle. Spectre, the AC-130 gunship, was operational.

Earlier gunship conversions from transport aircraft had been used successfully in Vietnam. The first was the Douglas AC-47 Spooky, which proved the gunship concept. Ironically, the idea came from a method practised by missionary aircraft in South America. To pick up mail from Christian outposts in the Amazon jungle, a pouch on a thin rope would be lowered while the aircraft, usually a light Cessna, was held in a tight turn over the outpost. The pouch would remain static at the centre of the turn radius, allowing the missionary on the ground to receive and "post" mail. It was a neat reversal of the control-line model aeroplane theory.

Side-firing guns were originally proposed by Lt Col G. C. MacDonald in 1942, for use against submarines. MacDonald later suggested a side-firing bazooka for use against tanks. Both ideas were rejected. In December 1961 MacDonald met Ralph Flexman, an engineer from Bell Aerosystems who was studying airborne counter-insurgency. MacDonald again suggested side-firing weapons, and Flexman's interest was aroused. After much ear-bending and fighting for funds the first flight test was carried out with a Convair C-151 fitted with one of the new General Electric SUU-11A 7.62 mm rotary-barrel gun pods. The weapon, with

Rolling into a firing orbit, this AC-130A first feels out the target with its 20 mm rotary cannon. Note the lack of inboard tanks and the empty outboard pylons. On AC-130s these hardpoints could carry tanks, flares or bombs. "Spooky" made a comeback in the invasion of Grenada, knocking out several flak positions and machine-gun posts. (USAF)

a two-speed electric drive and Gatling-type barrels, was capable of firing 3,000 or 6,000 rounds per minute. The gun was bolted to the floor, facing out of the cargo door. The first test firings proved MacDonald's idea beyond a doubt.

Full funding for the project was quickly approved, and in 1964 a C-47 was pulled out of mail-run duties with the 1st Air Commando Squadron at Nha Trang and modified to carry three SUU-11s aimed via a port-side-mounted gunsight from a Douglas A-1 Skyraider. After several missions the FC-47, as it was then designated, acquired the nickname "Puff the Magic Dragon". The Vietcong called it the Dragonship, from the howling stream of fire it breathed. Fighter pilots, however, were not happy about the "F" designation. When their howls of indignation at being put on par with C-47 "Truckie" pilots echoed through the Pentagon's corridors, the designation was changed to AC-47 – A for attack. When the first AC-47 unit, the 4th Air Commando Squadron, became operational in early 1966, the unit was assigned the tactical callsign "Spooky".

The Spooks soon became popular with US Army troops on the ground because of the gunships' ability to remain on station for hours, providing heavy, accurate and demoralizing firepower when needed. The Army wanted more, bigger and better-armed gunships. For Gunship II the Air Force looked for a reliable airframe with plenty of room for growth. It selected the C-130, but the Hercs were sorely needed at the time to haul cargo. An interim solution was the Fairchild AC-119 Shadow, the gunship version of the twin-boom Flying Boxcar transport. The Shadows held the fort in Vietnam as Gunship III until enough Hercules could be spared for conversion to AC-130As.

The Gunship II or AC-130 programme was built on the experience gained with the AC-47s. The larger Hercules was able to carry more armament, and four General Electric 7.62 mm MXU-470 modules were fitted, plus four General Electric M-61 20 mm rotary cannon originally designed for fighters. On the C-130A prototype they were mounted on the starboard side, with two 20 mm cannon and two 7.62 mm guns forward of the main undercarriage and a similar arrangement aft of the gear.

To aid target location and identification the AC-130 was fitted with a 20 kW searchlight, an infrared sensor, and an

adaptation of the infantry's low-light-level image-intensifier device popularly known as the Starlight Scope. A "brass-board" computer calculated bank angle, windage and recoil-induced-yaw corrections, eliminating pilot "guesstimation".

The prototype, a converted C-130A, was tested at Eglin AFB, Florida, in the summer of 1967. Two crews were trained to operate the aircraft, and on 20 September, 1967, they arrived at Nha Trang AB to carry out operational evaluation in South Vietnam. After a couple of missions supporting US and South Vietnamese troops in the "in-country" war, the C-130 crew obtained permission to go truck-hunting along the Ho Chi Minh Trail on 9 November, and set six trucks ablaze in 15 min. Having proved the concept with the C-130A prototype, the USAF awarded Ling-Temco-Vought a contract to convert seven JC-130As into AC-130A gunships.

The armament of the AC-130s was four 20 mm and four 7.62 mm guns, as on the prototype, but the target location and designation systems were improved. A Texas Instruments AN/AAD-4 forward-looking infrared (FLIR) was mounted in a small ball turret in the forward section of the port main gear sponson. The FLIR would scan for targets, picking up the difference in temperature produced by engine or body heat. When locked into the guns' boresight it could also be used to aim the guns. Another target location and aiming device was a Texas Instruments moving target indicator (MTI) radar. As the name implies, an MTI shows only moving echoes, ignoring stationary objects such as huts or trees.

Both the radar and FLIR fed target information to a Singer computer which then passed data to the pilot's side-facing head-up display (HUD). This showed the pilot where the target was and how to manoeuvre the AC-130 to obtain a first-run hit.

The eight AC-130s, including the prototype, were old airframes. Because of the punishment of low-level, high-energy manoeuvring, coupled with the recoil-induced stress of firing broadsides, they suffered a low serviceability rate at first. Part of the problem was that each aircraft was slightly different, compounding the spares and servicing problems of its many complex systems. Four of the seven AC-130As were sent to Vietnam in 1968. The other three remained at Eglin to train crews until the new 16th SOS was formed at Ubon Royal Thai Air Force Base in May 1969.

Meanwhile, the Gunship II programme progressed on to Project Surprise Package. Another C-130A was converted into AC-130 configuration, but with the rear pair of 20 mm Gatlings replaced by two quick-firing 40 mm Bofors cannon, originally designed as anti-aircraft guns. The rear pair of 7.62 mm guns were also removed. In their place was fitted a General Electric ASQ-145 Low Light Level TV (LLLTV) camera and a Motorola APQ-133 side-looking radar.

Another addition was a Korad AN/AVQ-18 laser rangefinder/designator. Using the AVQ-18, AC-130s could now pinpoint and "illuminate" ground targets for aircraft carrying laser-guided bombs or missiles. A video recorder was linked into the LLLTV and FLIR systems, allowing the crew to "re-run" their mission at debrief. The computer was changed for a faster-acting digital type with a larger memory and better software. The Surprise Package aircraft represented a quantum jump in effectiveness, and nine more were converted to AC-130s by LTV. This latest AC-130A variant was dubbed Pave Pronto, earlier AC-130s being unkindly called Plain Janes.

Pave Pronto was the same as Surprise Package but for one additional system, Black Crow. This device picked up unsuppressed ignition systems on truck engines, just like a domestic TV, but Black Crow gave the bearing of the ignition. Unfortunately for Charlie all of his Russian Zil trucks had unsuppressed ignition systems – it was a sneaky trick, but very effective. The first Pave Pronto Hercs deployed to "Nam" in December 1970, and the Plain Janes, by now down to six, were sent back to the United States for rebuild to Pave Pronto standard.

All of the AC-130As were old airframes, and under Pave Pronto were carrying as much equipment as possible. The excrescences housing the sensors made the usually clean Hercules "draggy". The early-model Allison engines were labouring to lift the heavy load from Vietnam's hot and humid airfields. When the aircraft were flying at low level the drag and weight increases put the fuel consumption up and the endurance fell. Finally the USAF decided to use later-model C-130Es to update its gunship fleet and allow performance margins for future developments.

Eleven C-130s, all low-time aircraft, were taken from cargo-hauling service for conversion to AC-130E Pave Spectre standard. All AC-130Es had the basic weapons and systems fit of the Pave Pronto models but carried more armour, fuel and ammunition. In addition a blister observation dome was fitted to the cargo ramp, allowing the Illumination Operator (IO) or "flarekicker" to watch for hostile ground fire or SAM launches. On the earlier models the kicker had to lie on the open ramp with his head over the edge. Besides being safer for the IO, the closed ramp improved the aerodynamics, giving better range and endurance. The first AC-130Es arrived at Ubon, Thailand, on 25 October, 1971.

To enable the Spectres to stand off from heavily defended targets and to knock out tanks, which were now coming south in increasing numbers, the USAF decided to upgun the AC-130E. After evaluating several heavy guns and recoilless launchers, the programme office at Wright-Patterson chose the US Army's 105 mm howitzer. With a flat-trajectory slant range of 1,200 m, the 105 allowed the Spectre to lob 44 lb shells accurately while staying beyond the range of Charlie's 57 mm AAA, usually the heaviest type found defending the Trail.

Mounted in place of one of the 40 mm Bofors in the rear paratroop door, the 105 mm gun was extremely successful. Original 105 mm mounts were rigid, and were later changed for a trainable mount. The gun was directed by the fire-control computer, using a similar gyro system to that of the British Chieftain tank to keep the gun on target, automatically compensating for the sometimes rough ride at low level. All AC-130Es were eventually retrofitted with the 105 mm weapon, but the AC-130A Pave Prontos retained the Bofors.

The various standards of Hercules gunship, from AC-130A (**top left**) to howitzer-equipped AC-130E (**bottom right**).

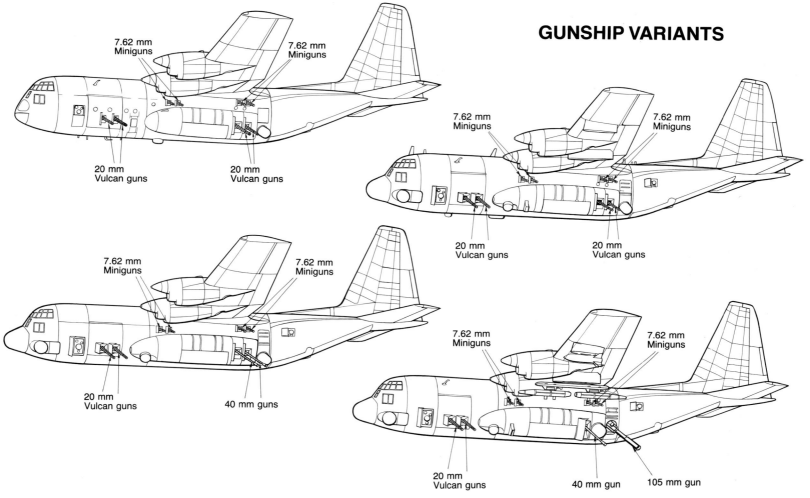

GUNSHIP VARIANTS

7.62 mm Miniguns

7.62 mm Miniguns

20 mm Vulcan guns

20 mm Vulcan guns

7.62 mm Miniguns

7.62 mm Miniguns

20 mm Vulcan guns

20 mm Vulcan guns

7.62 mm Miniguns

7.62 mm Miniguns

20 mm Vulcan guns

40 mm guns

7.62 mm Miniguns

7.62 mm Miniguns

20 mm Vulcan guns

40 mm gun

105 mm gun

When the USAF upgraded the C-130E fleet in 1972, fitting new avionics and more powerful Allison T-56A-15 engines instead of T-56A-7s, the AC-130E force was included. The designation was changed from AC-130E to AC-130H and all aircraft were rationalized, being given exactly the same standard of equipment. The first AC-130H Pave Spectre to return to Vietnam deployed to Ubon in March 1973.

Vietnam saw the birth of the Hercules gunship and the USAF still retains the AC-130s on Air Force Reserve squadrons. The service planned to use two AC-130s to provide covering fire during the withdrawal from the Tehran rescue mission. In the event, tragedy overtook the rescue fleet on the way to the target and the gunships were not used – something for which the citizens of Tehran can be truly thankful. But they did go into action once more in 1983, suppressing enemy fire during the Grenada operation.

Carolina Moon and the Dragon's Jaw

US Navy strike attack crews operating over North Vietnam in the mid-sixties got to know the Route Package system well. A Route Package (RP) was one of six arbitrary areas into which North Vietnam was divided in November 1965. The US Navy and US Air Force were given responsibility for three RPs each.

To the Navy fell RP IV, which contained the Thanh Hoa bridge, an important link in North Vietnam's logistics chain. Opened in 1964 and built of steel and concrete, the Thanh Hoa Bridge was 56 ft wide and 540 ft long, carried a railway line and a 22 ft-wide concrete road down each side, and stood 50 ft above the Song Ma river. It rested on a concrete pier in the river centre and concrete abutments at each end. As the war progressed and attacks on the bridge intensified, eight additional concrete piers were added. The bridge was known to the Vietnamese as Ham Rong, or Dragon's Jaw.

The first strike against the Dragon's Jaw was made on 3 April, 1965. Named Rolling Thunder-9-Alpha, the strike was made up of 46 F-105D Thunderchiefs and 21 F-100 Super Sabres, backed up by ten KC-135 Stratotankers with two photo-reconnaissance RF-101 Voodoos to run a post-strike battle damage assessment. Two Bullpup missiles per aircraft were loaded on 16 of the F-105s. The other 30 carried eight 750 lb bombs each. Fifteen of the F-105s were to go for the bridge; the rest would join seven of the F-100s in flak suppression. Eight more F-100s would provide cover for search and rescue helicopters should they be needed, and four Super Sabres would fly top cover, keeping watch for enemy fighters. The remaining two F-100s would arrive over the target first, giving a last-minute update of the weather conditions.

The missile-armed F-105s attacked first, followed rapidly by the dive-bomb attack. After the smoke cleared the bridge was intact. Most of the bombs and missiles had hit, but damage was minimal. One of the roadways was out of action for a few days, but apart from that and some charred paintwork and twisted metal, the Thanh Hoa bridge was serviceable. Two aircraft were lost on the first attack.

The Dragon's Jaw withstood many such conventional attacks by both the US Air Force and, later, when the Route Pack system came into being, the US Navy. The bridge was closed for repairs for a while after some strikes but never fell. The weapons were hitting the target, but they were too weak to knock it out.

In late 1965 the US Air Force Armament Development Laboratory invented a means of focusing the energy from an explosion into an instantaneous high-powered "jet". This jet of energy, lasting only milliseconds, was ideal for cutting through metal or concrete – or bridges. The focused-beam bomb was still in the experimental stage, however, and was too large to be carried by any strike aircraft then in service. Weighing 5,000 lb, the weapon was saucer-shaped, 9 ft in diameter and 2½ ft thick. A large aircraft was required to carry and drop the weapon, and the C-130 filled the bill.

The problem was delivery. A C-130 could not be expected to penetrate the extremely heavy, accurate and well-practised defences of the Thanh Hoa bridge. The answer was to drop the weapon just up-river and let it float downstream to the bridge. Magnetic sensors would detect the bridge's metal structure and detonate the secret weapon.

Two C-130s were adapted to drop the weapons and the crews were trained over Florida. Each aircraft was to drop five weapons. The route to the drop point would be flown at 100 ft, climbing to 400 ft and slowing to 145 kt for the drop. Two drop points were surveyed: the primary was about two miles upstream of the bridge and the secondary half that distance.

On 30 May, 1965, the first Hercules climbed out from Da Nang airfield with its 25,000 lb load of special weapons for Operation Carolina Moon. Heading out to sea, the Herc gradually dropped down to 100 ft before turning north. At about 0130 hr the C-130 crossed the North Vietnamese coast north of Thanh Hoa. The aircraft turned south, still at 100 ft, with the radio silent and the cockpit lights turned to their lowest setting. Two Phantoms attacked road and rail targets south of Thanh Hoa, attracting the attention of the North Vietnamese and drowning out the drone of the approaching Hercules. No ground fire was encountered on approaching the two-mile drop point, so the crew pressed on to the one-mile point, determined to release the weapons as close to the bridge as possible.

At this point the flak started to come up thick and fast, but the Hercules continued, aided by an EB-66 Skywarrior circling overhead, jamming the enemy target-acquisition radars. The five weapons were dropped accurately and the Hercules dived back below 100 ft, heading eastwards for the sea at top speed.

Next day, a photographic reconnaissance mission revealed that, once again, the Dragon's Jaw was unscathed. No trace of the weapons could be found. Perhaps they had sunk or missed the river completely – no one knows. The second Hercules and the last five bombs were prepared for a repeat mission the following night. Taking off from Da Nang after midnight, the Hercules followed the same route. The fate of the C-130 has never been explained. The Phantom crews, again flying a diversion raid, noted a large explosion near the bridge a few minutes before the Herc was due to drop the weapons. From information gained from a North Vietnamese prisoner, intelligence later reported that four of the five weapons had exploded on the first mission, but that the bridge was again undamaged.

Although battered and twisted by numerous heavy strikes, the Dragon's Jaw remained intact and operational until 14 May, 1972, when Phantoms eventually downed the west span with nine 3,000 lb laser-guided bombs. The Vietnamese were still repairing it when South Vietnam collapsed.

Combat Talon over Son Tay

In 1970 the United States of America was deeply embroiled in the Vietnam War. Its Air Force and Navy were striking targets in North Vietnam almost daily until President Johnson halted the bombing in October 1968. Almost 400 American aircrew were prisoners of war (POWs) in North Vietnamese camps, and almost 1,000 aircrew were listed as missing in action.

Of the POWs, some 70 were held at a camp just outside Son Tay, about 23 miles west of North Vietnam's capital, Hanoi. Many of the POWs were in bad shape both physically and mentally. After ejecting, which sometimes caused back injuries and limb dislocations, the aircrew were usually powerless to evade capture. Most aircrew were beaten severely, adding to their injuries. The first stop, and for many their last, was the infamous "Hanoi Hilton" – Hoa Lo prison, or its lesser known equivalent, Son Tay. Here the POWs were tortured for weeks at a time. Until a prisoner talked he was not fed. The food itself was a health hazard, being unfit for pigs, let alone humans. Contact between prisoners was usually minimal, consisting of messages tapped through walls.

Routine photographic reconnaissance coverage of the Son Tay area in early 1970 revealed what was thought to be a signal, the letter "K", tramped out in the soil. Not part of the standard international ground-to-air emergency code, K was sometimes used by US ground forces in South Vietnam to call in an airborne pick-up. The Strategic Air Command photo interpreters passed the information on to a special POW intelligence unit. Later signals photographed by Lockheed SR-71s appeared to show an arrow and the figure "8"

HH-3E refuels from an HC-130P tanker. The Son Tay raiders carried out this tricky manoeuvre – at night, within minutes of entering combat.

made up of drying laundry. The arrow pointed to Mount Ba Vi, located about eight miles south-west of Son Tay camp. What were the POWs trying to say?

The inference was that the POWs wanted a helicopter pick-up at Ba Vi. Perhaps, the intelligence net reasoned, the POWs visited the Ba Vi area on work parties? But when? An initial plan was formed to send in a Sikorsky HH-3 helicopter from Northern Laos on receipt of a signal from a Special Forces agent at Ba Vi, which would indicate that the prisoners were ready for pick-up.

The idea was put up for consideration. The conditions inside the camps were known to be harsh. Why not raid Son Tay and Ap Lo camps, which were both in the same area, and release dozens, maybe hundreds, of POWs? The Joint Chiefs of Staff approved of the idea, and it was then up to the then incumbent President, Richard Nixon. He agreed, and the Son Tay raid was on.

The raid was divided into three parts: infiltration, taking the camp, and the escape (or, in Pentagonese, "exfiltration"). The infiltration would be by helicopter. A Sikorsky HH-3E "Jolly Green Giant" or a Bell UH-1 would crash-land inside the prison compound. Two of five HH-53s

would lay down covering fire, one flying between the guard towers firing its port and starboard SUU-11 7.62 miniguns at 6,000 rounds per minute each. After the guards had been killed the prisoners would be hustled aboard the helicopters, which would then head back through the hills to Laos at low level.

Two MC-130E "Combat Talon" Hercules would guide the helicopters in and out. The Son Tay Combat Talon crews flew probably the most difficult C-130 mission ever conceived. The role of Combat Talon was, and is, shrouded in secrecy but basically a Combat Talon C-130 is fully equipped to infiltrate and evacuate special forces troops such as the US Green Berets or the British Special Air Service. Like its passengers, the Combat Talon is fully equipped to carry out a range of jobs, some of them straightforward, others falling into the "dirty tricks" category.

Another C-130, an HC-130P "Kingship" of the Aerospace Rescue and Recovery Service, would refuel the HH-53s before they crossed the Laos/North Vietnam border. The helicopters would then have the maximum amount of time available to ground-loiter if necessary.

One of the two Combat Talons would lead the

One of several variants designed for clandestine missions is the MC-130H. Until the advent of the RAF's probe-equipped Hercs this was the only model able to receive fuel in flight.

helicopter force on its low-level approach to Son Tay and then climb to illuminate the prison with parachute flares. The other was to guide the supporting strike force of Douglas A-1 Skyraiders around and under North Vietnam's extensive air defence radar system.

The problem for the Combat Talon aircrews was that the convoy of aircraft had to fly at the speed of the slowest aircraft. Inbound this was the HH-3, the largest helicopter able to squeeze into Son Tay. The compound was surrounded by trees on the inside of the wall, and the initial assault group was to lie on mattresses in the HH-3 as its crew flew it through the trees to crash-land in the compound. The HH-3's top speed was 105 kt. A C-130 normally cruises at 200–250 kt, and refuelling of helicopters by C-130s is regarded as "a bit squirly" at 125 kt. The Combat Talon crew had to maintain 105 kt, about 10 per cent above stalling speed.

The technique was to use 70 per cent flap and hang nose-high, with lots of power to "blow" the wing. Because the C-130 is not very responsive at such speeds and the autopilot is not sensitive enough for low-speed, low-altitude manoeuvring, the aircraft must be flown manually. Power handling must also be treated with great caution. An asymmetric application of power or the sudden loss of an engine would roll the Herc inverted in seconds. With the aircraft in a nose-high attitude the rudder was partly blanked and couldn't provide enough force with sufficient speed to counteract a dead engine and prevent a roll.

To make matters worse, the MC-130's terrain-following radar was pointed skywards by the nose-high attitude, limiting the radar picture to the bottom portion of its envelope. Radar warning of approaching obstacles would therefore be both limited and late. While one pilot would have to fly the aeroplane using the forward-looking infra-red (FLIR) system to pick out obstacles, the other would monitor attitude and airspeed, correcting the latter with small, gentle throttle inputs. The Hercules would be flying in what pilots call "coffin corner", approaching the back of the drag curve, where only the gentlest of control inputs can be used if disaster is to be avoided. The underpowered HH-3 would fly as close behind the MC-130 as possible, taking advantage of the Herc's "suction".

The second MC-130 would also be hampered. Although it would be flying at a more comfortable 140 kt to guide the Skyraiders, it had to be ready to take over if Number One flew into the ground, which was quite likely. The strike force would have an airspeed of 140 kt, but would maintain its mean speed along track at 105 kt by continuous S-turns and orbits. This was not an attractive proposition either, leading a large formation through constant turns at night, at low-level and in mountainous terrain while avoiding detection by the enemy. The flight would be made in strict radio silence and without lights. The two Combat Talon captains were Maj Irl Franklin of the 7th Special Operations Squadron and Lt Col Albert Blosch of the 1st Special Operations Wing. Franklin was to pilot the helicopter guide while Blosch flew the strike-force guide.

After months of practice, both in the air and on the ground, the Operation Kingpin team arrived at Takhli Royal Thai Air Force Base. The force now had to wait for last-minute clearance from Washington and for the right moonlight and weather conditions. The moon had to be just bright enough to see by, but not so bright as to make the aircraft easily seen. The visibility had to be good because visual navigation was to be used for most of the flight. Each MC-130E carried an extra navigator to share the workload. The air could not be too turbulent or the HH-53s could not link up with the HC-130 to refuel. Too strong a surface wind in the target area would hamper the helicopters. Moreover, a diversionary raid by carrier-based attack aircraft was planned, and moderate seas were needed in the Gulf of Tonkin for the launch and recovery of the strike aircraft. The weather over the port of Haiphong also had to be good for the diversionary sweep by the Navy A-7 Corsairs and F-8 Crusaders.

As it transpired, the raid was launched 24 hr early, on 20 November, 1980, to avoid a typhoon approaching North Vietnam across the sea. The weather en route and over Son Tay was almost ideal. A C-130 transferred the special forces further north to Udorn airbase to meet the three HH-53s and an HH-3 which were to take them in and the two HH-53s equipped with medical kits that would evacuate the POWs. The two Combat Talon MC-130s also departed, one for Udorn and the other for Nakon Phanom to meet the A-1 strike force.

After some trouble starting an engine the MC-130 at Udorn left 23 min behind schedule, but it was easily able to catch up with the helicopters, which were meanwhile being guided by the HC-130 tanker. The two forces met over central Laos and headed slightly north of east for Son Tay, dropping down to take advantage of terrain masking. Out in the Gulf the carriers *Hancock, Oriskany* and *Ranger* launched their mixed force of A-7 Corsairs and F-8 Crusaders for Haiphong.

Less than one minute ahead of schedule Franklin and his crew in the Combat Talon Hercules pulled up and away from the helicopters with Son Tay dead on the nose at two miles range, the Song Con river bending around the prison and the lights of Hanoi visible beyond. Climbing into an orbit above the prison, they prepared to disrupt any North Vietnamese attempts to interfere with the raid.

First of all the MC-130 had to drop flares over the prison at a precise time, to aid the approach and crash of the HH-3 and destroy the prison guards' night vision. As the HH-3 approached the prison walls the flares exploded into brilliant white light overhead. The HH-53 dashed across the prison at roof level, minigun rounds pouring into the guard towers and the guards' quarters. It smashed its way through the trees amid a shower of leaves, branches, and rotor blades and thumped down in the compound. Fourteen Special Forces troops jumped from the wrecked helicopter and headed for the cell blocks.

Above, the Combat Talon crews opened their bag of tricks and played havoc with the North Vietnamese Army's (NVA) radio net. Scanning across the spectrum, the Combat Talons cruised around dropping flares and special weapons. On hitting the ground these weapons produced a series of small explosions simulating small-arms fire, including machine-gun noises. Any troops on the way to reinforce Son

Philippine Aerotransport's smart colour scheme enhances the L-100-20's lines. Note that civil models do not have the lower cockpit windows.

Tay's guards would naturally head for what sounded like a fire fight, only to have it apparently die down and then start again some miles away as the Combat Talon dropped another device. In case any NVA reinforcements got too close to Son Tay for comfort the Combat Talons were also carrying a mix of napalm and "daisy-cutter" cluster bombs on triple ejector racks under the wings. There was also the A-1 Skyraider force in reserve.

Back on the ground one of the HH-53s mistakenly put its load of troops down at a second compound about two miles south of Son Tay prison. Unfortunately this compound, thought by intelligence to be a school, was an NVA base. The 22 Special Forces troops were not deterred. As the North Vietnamese soldiers poured from their barracks they encountered heavy and accurate fire, and more than 100 of them were killed before the HH-53 picked up its troops and jumped them across to the real target.

However, when the Kingpin force looked into the cells at Son Tay they met the one contingency that no one had planned for. The cells were empty. Some months previously the Song Con river had risen and threatened to burst its banks and flood the adjacent prison. The NVA had abandoned Son Tay and moved the prisoners to other camps. Although the raid was a complete success in military terms, it was one of the most serious intelligence blunders in recent years.

Nearly ten years later the Combat Talon Hercules, the HH-53s and the Green Berets were to meet again. This time, in Iran, the mission went terribly wrong. First, several of the helicopters went unserviceable. Then a devastating crash occurred. As a CH-53 manoeuvred to take on fuel from a C-130 at the Desert One covert base its rotor downwash, coupled with the propwash from the Herc, caused it to roll until its main rotor hit the C-130's fuselage. In the ensuing fire and explosion, a number of men were killed and several aircraft were damaged. The C-130 and CH-53 were burnt out.

The mission commander was forced to withdraw his force. Ironically, on this occasion the hostages were exactly where they were expected to be – in the American Embassy in Tehran. But Son Tay had proved the feasibility of the Tehran raid.

Airlift on the civil scene

Lockheed soon realized that the civil airfreight market was suffering from a lack of purpose-built cargo aircraft of the C-130's calibre. The company proposed the GL-207, a slightly different aircraft from the military Hercules which was rolling off the line at Marietta.

The GL-207 model was to be larger than the C-130B, with 23 ft 4 in greater length and the wingspan increased by 12 ft 5 in. The power would be supplied by 6,000 shp Allison T-61s, allowing a maximum take-off weight of 204,170 lb. Pan American took options on 12 GL-207s, scheduled for delivery in 1962. Slick Airways was to follow with six GL-207s, also for 1962 delivery.

Two more powerful versions of the GL-207 were also proposed. One was to be driven by four 6,445 shp Rolls-Royce Tynes and would weigh in at 230,000 lb, and the other was really a new aeroplane, being powered by four 22,000 lb-thrust Pratt & Whitney JT3D-11 turbofan engines. This aircraft would have had a gross weight of 250,000 lb.

However, the two launch customers cancelled their options. Faced with the choice of building the new version as a private venture or modifying the standard, proven Hercules for civil certification, Lockheed chose the latter, less expensive route. All civil variants are based on the military design with suitable modifications and growth as dictated by market demands.

The civil Hercules is built in three basic models. The first to fly was the L-100, which made a record-breaking maiden flight of 25 hr and 1 min, begun on 20 April, 1961. The L-100 is powered by Allison 501-D22s, the civil equivalent of the Allison T56, producing 4,050 shp each.

The civil Hercules obtained Federal Aviation Administration certification in February 1965, and the first aircraft was delivered to Continental Air Services the following September. Twenty-one L-100s were eventually built besides the prototype. This and eight production airframes were later rebuilt as L-100-20s. Another pair were eventually stretched to L-100-30 standard.

One version of the C-130 which never got past the model stage was this amphibious proposal. Apart from the boat hull and tip floats, the engines are inverted, *à la* P-3C Orion, and mounted above the wing for increased prop-tip clearance and to avoid spray ingestion. A flying scale model was successfully tested.

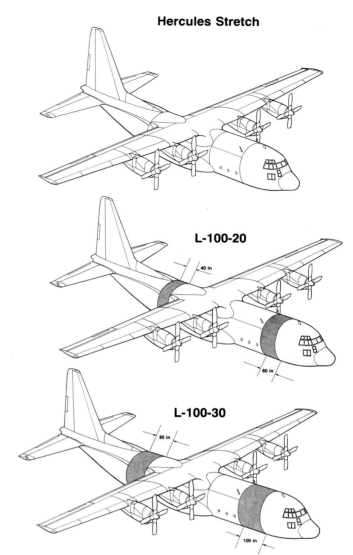

Hercules Stretch

L-100-20

L-100-30

The two Hercules stretches compared with (**top**) the standard airframe.

In 1967 it was becoming apparent that, successful as the L-100 was, the market needed a larger version with greater cargo space. Although many of the civil operations involved lifting heavy loads, just as many involved the transport of light but bulky high-value cargo. Thus the civil variant could "bulk out" with low-mass, high-volume cargoes. Lockheed decided to stretch the aircraft, increasing the cargo space while keeping the maximum take-off weight at the 155,000 lb of the L-100.

Two "plugs" were inserted into the fuselage. One, 5 ft long, was inserted forward of the wing, while another of 3 ft 4 in was built in aft of the wing. This fairly simple modification gave a cargo hold volume of 5,307 ft³, compared with the 4,500 ft³ of the L-100. The L-100-20, which was also available with 4,500 shp Allison 501-D22A engines, was certificated in October 1968 and entered service with Interior Airways the same month. Lockheed built 25 L-100-20s in addition to the nine L-100s rebuilt to the stretched standard.

A further stretch, the L-100-30, first flew in 1970. This time the cargo hold volume was increased to 6,057 ft³ by stretching the fuselage another 6 ft 8 in. The engine choice and maximum take-off weight remained the same as for the L-100-20. This variant made its commercial debut in 1970 with Saturn Airways.

The L-100-30 was originally dubbed the Super Hercules by Lockheed, but the name does not appear to have caught on, "Stretch Herc" or "Dash 30" being more common. The aircraft has a clear cubic cargo volume 9 ft high, 10 ft wide and 55 ft long, plus a load-stressed ramp. With an average cargo density of 101 lb/ft³ the 60,570 lb payload falls into the correct density/volume, load/range profitability figures for many civil operators' company accountants.

Typical loads for civil Hercules include the normal stuff of publicity brochures such as bulldozers and drilling and mining equipment. An increasingly common load in these days of industrial offsets and international co-operation is aircraft parts. But the fully pressurized air-conditioned hold has also proved useful in transporting livestock. This normally ranges from pedigree cattle to day-old chicks, but more exotic species have been carried, including bears, porpoises, racehorses, giraffes (the means is a mystery), elephants, rhinoceros, lions, tigers and the odd killer whale.

It is not livestock alone that benefits from the controlled-environment hold. Delicate electronic equipment can be sent by Hercules, unloaded and used immediately without the need for recalibration because of temperature and pressure extremes.

The L-100-30 is a moneyspinner when it is used correctly, and that means being airborne as long and as often as possible. In commercial flying an aircraft "down" for unserviceability is a liability rather than an asset. The Hercules is both rugged and reliable, while being simple to maintain away from base. It is also relatively quiet to operate, and can sneak in and out of civil airports late at night without upsetting local residents. Thus the Herc-equipped carrier can take urgent loads where a competing company's noisier turbojet aircraft, which looks quicker on paper, is banned from landing or taking off before times specified by local noise regulations.

Remember the original Hercules specification – the bit about a clear-cargo volume similar to a railroad boxcar?

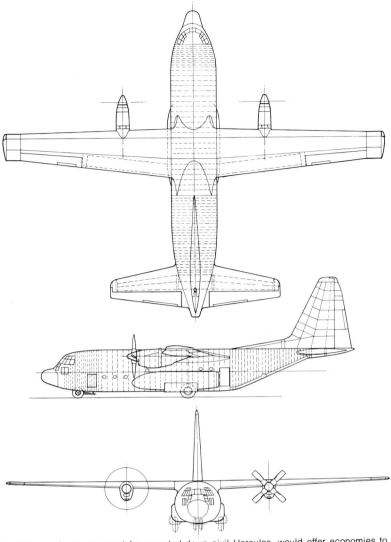

L-400, Lockheed's proposal for a scaled-down civil Hercules, would offer economies to commercial operators.

One of the many civil Hercules operators is Air Algérie, which uses its L-100-30s on desert oil support tasks.

Well, the US Air Force hit upon the dimensions of the standard commercial cargo container some ten years before its invention. The L-100-30 can take two standard 8 ft × 8 ft × 20 ft containers (or one 40 ft long) plus one 10 ft-long container. Other aircraft common in the cargo field, such as the civil cargo/passenger widebodies, must have containerized loads repacked into smaller containers with relatively complex cross-sections to fit their below-floor cargo compartments. This slows down a shipment and makes the cargo, which is usually of high value if it merits air transport, vulnerable to pilfering or damage during handling. You do not need to be an accountant to see why the civil Hercules is as successful as its military counterparts.

Other commercial derivatives based on the L-100-30 have been proposed by Lockheed, but they have not yet found a strong enough market on which to base production of a prototype. These options include an even longer stretch of 20 ft in the L-100-50, the L-100-30PX 100-passenger aircraft, the "quick change" L-100-30QC passenger/cargo convertible with an easily fitted "people pod" containing seats and services, and the L-100-30C, a "half and half" combined passenger/cargo aircraft.

Perhaps the most promising variant proposed was the twin-engined L-400, which raised a flurry of interest and, strangely, derisory comment from a well-known company which was itself marketing a large twin-engined transport. Perhaps it was scared of the L-400's potential. The L-400 concept unfortunately coincided with the start of the recession, and the idea was shelved in 1980. However, it is worth remembering the L-400, as the project could well become viable in a better financial climate.

Lockheed's philosophy on the twin-engined L-400 is that the aircraft would be cheaper to buy and operate than the standard Hercules. While offering the same cargo hold size, 4,500 ft³, as the standard C-130, the L-400 would have a maximum payload, limited by engine power, of 25,000 lb. Typical payload/range figures for the twin Herc would be 20,500 lb over 550 nm or 15,000 lb over 1,400 nm.

Of the same overall shape, the L-400 would be powered by two Allison 501-D22D engines of 4,591 shp each. These would be fitted with 14 ft-diameter auto-feathering propellers and water-methanol injection, both of these features being new to the Hercules range. The latter would improve take-off performance in the heavy/hot/high case. The fuselage, tail and most of the wing would be the same as those of the C-130, giving spares commonality. The only major changes would be a shorter wing centre-section allied to C-130H outer wings with new, 4½ ft-longer wing tips. The new wing would span 119 ft. Obviously the inboard trailing-edge flaps would be eliminated along with the inboard engines. The maximum take-off weight would be 84,000 lb, compared with the C-130H's 155,000 lb.

The L-400's cockpit would be different, catering for two-crew operation (civil L-100s have a three-man crew, and military C-130s usually have a crew of five). The lower gross weight allows the deletion of one of the main wheels on each side, although the L-400 could operate from the same surfaces as the heavier, four-engined models. The fuel system would be simpler than the C-130's, with no external tankage and 30,000 lb capacity in two main and two auxiliary tanks. With both civil and military versions designed, the L-400 might yet go into production.

Marshall of Cambridge and Flight Refuelling Ltd reacted quickly when the Royal Air Force needed to refuel its Hercules during the Falklands War. From the initial idea to this, the first dry prod, took two weeks. Tanker is a Victor K.2.   (MoD)

Falklands lift

In 1982 the Royal Air Force Hercules fleet was engaged in, and bore the brunt of, the service's largest logistics operation since the Berlin Airlift. Argentina invaded the Falkland Islands, and Great Britain was determined to regain them. While the naval Task Force, including the carriers *Hermes* and *Invincible*, put to sea amid a wave of publicity on 3 April, the C-130 force at Lyneham was secretly swinging into action.

The nearest British territory to the Falklands is Ascension Island, 3,900 miles north, off the west coast of Africa. A good airfield, Wideawake, is maintained there by the US Air Force to resupply the US satellite tracking station on Ascension. It was to this airfield, some 4,100 miles south of Britain, that Lyneham's Hercules squadrons flew tons of cargo.

First into Ascension was the Mobile Air Movements Squadron. Its years of practice loading, unloading and sorting cargo in exercises was about to be put to the test in a real confrontation. Another little-known RAF unit, 38 Group's Tactical Communications Wing, also flew in to set up Tacan beacons, HF communications and an airmobile control tower to supplement the USAF's equipment and to provide secure communications with the United Kingdom and with the rapidly approaching Royal Navy Task Force.

Meanwhile the Lyneham Wing, comprising 24, 30, 47 and 70 Squadrons, was flying around the clock transporting tons of equipment, first to set up a tented base area at Wideawake and then to bring in stores, spares and ammunition for the Task Force. From Wideawake the equipment was shuttled out to the ships by helicopter, topping off reserves of ammunition and missiles for the coming battle. The pre-Falklands aircraft movements at Wideawake had increased tenfold, from 40 a day to 400. Most of them were Hercules, backed by VC10s of 10 Squadron for personnel transport.

Having moved a large amount of cargo to resupply the Task Force, the Hercules force then set up a continuous line of supply to avoid the two-week shipment by sea needed to reach Ascension. By 21 April the Hercules were flying south from Ascension almost daily to drop urgently needed spares, computer software changes and mail to the Task Force.

As the range increased the aircraft's payload capability dropped. Aided by Flight Refuelling Ltd, Marshalls of Cambridge and the Royal Aircraft Establishment, the RAF fitted an experimental refuelling probe to a C-130. The equipment was flight-tested on 3 May and the first probe-equipped Hercules arrived at Ascension on 4 May. The final flight test and clearance was made on 10 May. This extremely rapid modification was completed just in time. By 16 May the round trip to the Task Force and back took 26 hr.

Meanwhile, the RAF's Victor tanker force was hard pressed to keep up with its growing number of customers in the form of Harriers, Sea Harriers, Vulcans, Nimrods, Phantoms and Hercules. The decision was taken to equip four Hercules and six Vulcans as tankers. The programme went ahead at full speed, but was completed too late for the modified aircraft to see service in the South Atlantic. However, the Victors used up a lot of their airframe time during the Falklands conflict, and the Hercules tankers will supplement the new VC10 tanker fleet as the Victors retire.

Following the Argentine surrender the Hercules continued resupply flights to Port Stanley, first by air drop and later by landing on the airfield. The Hercs were refuelled twice at points 1,200 miles and 2,500 miles south of Ascension. In the "long slot" refuelling the C-130s take on up to 50,000 lb of fuel. In the South Atlantic campaign the Hercules fleet put in 13,000 hr of flying, lifting some 7,000 tons of cargo, 5,500 personnel, 100 vehicles and 20 helicopters.

As usual, the Hercules set another record. On 18 June a 70 Squadron Hercules captained by Flt Lt Terry Locke took off from Ascension to make a drop on East Falkland. On 19 June Locke's crew touched down at Ascension after an incredible 28 hr 3 min flight, the Hercules' longest flight yet and another episode in the life story of Lockheed's remarkable transport.